Don't Wait for the Green Light

by Andy Kahle

Copyright © 2020 by Andrea Kahle

All rights reserved. This book or any portion thereof may not be reproduced or used in any manner whatsoever without the express written permission of the publisher

except for the use of brief quotations in a book review.

First Printing, 2020

For any enquiries or permissions,
the Author can be contacted at andy@andyk.com.au

Edited By: Shoma Mittra - Write Click Writing Services

Cover Design & Illustration by: Andy Kahle - AndyK Design

ISBN: 978-0-6489044-0-3

*Thank you
to everyone who helped me get here ...
I couldn't have done it
without the support of so many.
:)*

Foreword

When you come out of a storm, you will never be the same person who walked in. That is the nature of storms.

'Don't Wait For The Green Light' is a profoundly moving story about Andy Kahle and her walk through her very own and very personal storm. The book is a remarkable and insightful journey of a survivor's courageous battle to beat the odds against breast cancer.

Andy pulls no punches as she relates in concise and readable language, generously sprinkled with her unique wry humour, the emotional and often unpredictable roller coaster ride she suddenly finds herself strapped into. Life as she knows it is about to spin totally out of her grasp.

Here is a very practical and amazingly independent woman who is happiest seated behind the wheel of a fast car, foot hard on the accelerator and feeling in total control of herself and of her surroundings.

Suddenly, without warning, her life spirals out of its happy and comfortable orbit and soars completely out of her control. Other people step in and take charge. Well-meaning but, nevertheless, other people are now sitting behind the wheel making the decisions and Andy is the passenger not quite sure what is happening and where exactly she is heading.

Almost from the very beginning, when Andy is first informed of her cancer and of this most unwanted, irritating interruption to her happy, busy life, she comes to the realisation that she has little choice but to pull out all the stops and focus her energy into getting better.

'You only get one life, and it's pretty short. Make the best of it. Don't let anything hold you back, not even breast cancer.' Andy's own words ...

With both eyes wide open and focused on the not so far away future where new beginnings patiently await, Andy, supported by her wonderful hubby, loving family, loyal friends and a very committed and dedicated medical team head into the storm to do battle.

In Andy's own words, 'I do consider myself lucky for having had this experience. I can see what I'm supposed to do with my life now and how to enjoy every single minute of it.'

Andy, you are my inspiration.
My love always.
Auntie Margie

Chapter 1
I Guess I just Won Lotto

People like me don't win lotto. People like me aren't on the news for doing something profound and amazing. People like me don't travel the world meeting up with celebrities and blogging about it.

People like me don't get breast cancer.

Well, that's what I thought anyway. I know you hear it on the news all the time about the sad loss of a celebrity after her brave struggle with cancer. It makes major headlines, and everyone starts talking about people they know who've had cancer. But that's not me. I didn't have any family history of cancer or even know anyone with cancer, at least not regular people like me. After all, I'm just a regular girl, living an ordinary married, suburban life, trying to etch out a meagre living in my own graphic design business, and life-threatening stuff like cancer doesn't enter the lives of people like me.

So how wrong was I? Not about being regular and ordinary. I'm still pretty ordinary, even if I do drag race a sub 9 second, V8 classic muscle car. I found out the hard way that regular people like me get cancer too, you just don't hear about it as much.

So let me welcome you into our little suburban house as an inconspicuous fly on the wall. This could be any day of the week, but it just so happens to be specifically Monday night, 22nd of March 2010.

"I'm just off to have a shower ... do you want me to yell out when I'm done so you can jump straight in?" I said as I walked past Mick, who was lying on the couch watching sport on TV. Our two dogs, Avey and Peppa, raised their heads, apprehensive about the word 'shower'.

No doubt they could have used a wash, but with everything planned for the upcoming Easter long weekend, it simply was not on the agenda.

"Yeh, thanks babe. I'll be in shortly ... I just want to catch the end of the news. There's a bit about Vermeulen and whether he's going to be back after his accident and race Superbike in Portugal. So, keep it warm for me." Mick is not just a sports nut, but a fully-fledged motor racing enthusiast, which is why making the decision to buy our own drag racing car, after many years helping out with everyone else's, wasn't a difficult one to make at all.

Just as the decision about who would drive the car wasn't a difficult one either. Mick likes to build and work on engines, and I like to drive. The idea of driving excessively fast is a thrill for me. We're the perfect match.

As I was about to lean out of the shower to call Mick in before the hot water ran out, I spotted him in the doorway, jiggling about in all his glory.
"It's getting cold standing out here, are you letting me in or what?"

So, I stepped aside, tweaking his butt cheeks as we did the '2 people in one little shower' waltz, trying not to slip up on the soapy surface.

Slipping in the shower was one situation we did not want to revisit. We had already delayed our drag racing debut by a season when Mick had managed to slip and impale himself on the shower tap. And yes, I did say 'impale'. That just happened to be the night before our intended first track meet.

We had ended a couple of very late nights preparing the drag car for my first track outing when Mick called out, all very casually from the bathroom.

"Andy, can you come here?"

So casual was his call out that I figured he had just forgotten to grab a fresh towel. Little did I realise, until I opened the bathroom door and saw him standing in the shower/bath with blood pouring out from under his arm, that it was a tad more serious.

Mick had caused himself such a unique injury slipping in the bath and impaling his bicep on the shower tap, that the ambulance attendants asked if they could take photographs of his wound. No doubt so they could share the story with their co-workers, which Mick also still does, but without the photos.

This was the second "sign" telling us we weren't going to be racing right away, the first being earlier that week when I blew up the transmission, while practising my drag racing launch technique in Gonzo's workshop carpark.

Then while we were coming back from one of Mick's doctor appointments - and because sometimes I run my mouth off before I engage my brain - I oddly announced that it should probably now be my turn. After all, Mick had already had his fair share; with an ankle reconstruction, retinal detachment, and now plastic surgery on his bicep.

"What?" Mick was shocked at my comment.

"I don't mean anything sinister; I just mean it must be my turn for you to look after me, in sickness and in health and all that," I replied. I was hardly ever sick and had only had an emergency room visit from some stitches after a motorcycle accident.

Boy, did that comment come back to bite me. Is it too late to take it back?

"Hon, I noticed something different about my boob while I was in the shower," I blurted out. I'm not a softly softly type person, and neither is Mick. Besides, I'd had lumps on my boobs before, so there was no reason for us to be alarmed. In fact, the thought of cancer didn't even cross my mind. I just didn't think to associate a lump in my breast to the possibility of breast cancer. For me, it was just a lump where there shouldn't be a lump.

Last time I had a lump, the doctor explained that I had very fibrous breast tissue, which is normally something you lose with age. I'm not sure if this is something I should be proud of, like having fewer wrinkles, but it did mean I'd end up with the occasional cyst. So, this was just a lump, no big deal, just something that had to be dealt with.

"Can you have a feel and tell me if I should get Dr Mark to have a look? Maybe I should just leave it for another week and see if it goes away."

I was starting to feel like a total drama queen and wished I hadn't even mentioned it. It didn't seem very big, and with everything we'd just been through with Mick's arm, I felt we didn't need any more drama in our life at that time.

"You'll have to direct where you think it is," Mick changed from jovial to serious in the blink of an eye. His big calloused diesel mechanic hands don't have the same sensitivity as my artist hands, and I could see that he was worried he wouldn't be able to find anything. I felt about, pointed to the spot and then felt a sudden shock at finding it again so quickly. Perhaps it was a little bigger than I first thought. But there was no pain, so I was thinking there's no infection, so therefore there's no hurry to deal with it.

"Yeeehhhhhhhh!" He sighed in his tired, 'I'm feigning disinterest so as not to cause alarm', the way that he does so well. "It won't hurt to go and get it checked out. Like you said, it's probably nothing."

It was going to be a very busy week already without trying to squeeze in doctor appointments and a mammogram, but I would make sure I got it checked.
With the Easter weekend looming, we had decided to have a busy bee to make room for a massive race shed in our backyard. It just didn't make sense for us to keep taking

up space in Gonzo's workshop when we had the space at home, and it would be much nicer to have the car here to show off to visitors.

I had to measure and stake out the back yard to calculate the size shed we would be able to fit, and finish drawing up the plans so we could get an accurate quote from the builders. And besides, I'm quite the control freak, so instead of getting someone in to do it, I'd much rather do all the planning myself. I also had two logos to finish for a couple of my clients, and three websites to design that I hadn't even started to think about, but which needed to be finished "before the long weekend". Even though being self-employed and working from home has its benefits, and business was booming, work sometimes felt as if it impinged on real life. I just like to cram so much stuff into my life, hobbies, work, friends and family to catch up, there's just not enough hours in a day or days in a week.

That night I fell into a deep sleep next to Mick and the dogs snoring under the bed, with a self-satisfied smile on my face, and forgot all about the lump in my breast. Instead I dreamed of our newly purchased drag racing car sitting on the hoist in a great big American barn style shed in our backyard, and the pending excitement of becoming an actual drag racer.

It was going to be such a fantastic weekend, with family and friends all coming over to help rip up the garden. I don't know what I was looking forward to more, the fun of everyone working together, or the imagined final result.

Life really is what you make it, and Mick and I were doing a pretty good job of making the most of it, even though it was just the two of us in our little family. We had a shared dream, and we were working hard to achieve it. The plan was just not to let anything muck it up even if there had been a few minor setbacks along the way with Mick's health. These problems just made us stronger and closer and made us strive harder to get every moment of enjoyment out of life.

Chapter 2
There's no Nice Way to Squish Boobs

I had a simple thought while glancing around the waiting room, waiting for only my second mammogram in four years. Why do waiting rooms only have women's gossip magazines? What do the blokes read when they come to get scanned for this or that or accompany their wives? I'm sure the only reason blokes hate going to the doctor is because there's nothing decent to read in the waiting room.

After accompanying me for multiple visits to the breast clinic, Mick decided to donate a big pile of motoring magazines to their waiting room, in the hope that he was better catering to the needs of the supportive hubby.

"They need a better class of distraction," he explained to me after he dumped his first donation on the waiting room table.

I do have to admit that we may have started a trend though, because since then I noticed that other visitors had been doing the same thing. My Breast Clinic is now proud to provide renovation, golfing, wrestling and financial advice magazines to accompany Micks motoring and the standard gossip magazines. There's even a small selection of teen and kids' magazines along with a few puzzles and toys to keep the little ones occupied while Mum waits for her appointment.

After spending so much time in waiting rooms, I have now found that the magazines just don't hold my attention, so I invested in a Kindle. It's great, it simply slips into my handbag, and I get to choose what I'm going to read.

"Andrea?" the nurse snapped me out of my own little dream world inside my head and beckoned me to follow her into the depths beyond the waiting room. The rest of the waiting room looked up from their gossip magazines briefly, confirmed someone had responded to the nurse's call, thus moving them closer to their appointment, and then went back to their own reading.

If you don't already know this firsthand, I'm sure you've heard that having a mammogram is not a very pleasant experience, and certainly not the most dignified. Whilst the nurses are lovely and try to explain the process in some detail, you cannot effectively be prepared the first time you have a mammogram. No-one can fully prepare you for the sight of your breasts being "squished" between two icy cold plates of glass as if you decided to take a drunken photocopy at the office Christmas party. Although I haven't done this personally, it is not something I would recommend doing in place of the professional mammogram due to unreliable results.

The most important thing to remember about having a test done is the requirement to wear the appropriate attire and I don't just mean the open-in-the-front version of the gown you wear in the hospital. If you make the mistake of wearing a dress, or even a bodysuit to your mammogram, you'll find yourself having to strip off all the way, but if you keep it simple with an easy on and off button up shirt, you'll find the experience a little less revealing.

I was directed into the tiny change room to switch my work shirt to a front opening, wrap around, 70s style, floral blouse which did nothing for my looks even in the mood lighting of the mammography room. Most of the breast clinics I've been to have a similar variation on the same design, tending only to change the colour or the length of the gown.

The absolute fashion winner in my personal opinion would have gone to one of the many different types of giant donut magnetic scanning machines I had the joy of visiting. After being handed a bright yellow, one size fits all, tracksuit made from a lightweight cotton I learnt to arrive sporting my own tracksuit in an equally fashionable gunmetal grey.

"Have you done this before?" the nurse asked, being quick with the small talk, as I removed the newly donned floral gown and headed over to the mammogram machine. She gently guided my body into the awkward stance of hugging what is essentially an x-ray machine, or if you prefer, an upside-down photocopier. She obviously realized that although I'm not happy about having a total stranger man-handle my boobs into position, before squishing them beyond recognition, I was pretty calm and relaxed about the whole experience of doing a gentle slow dance under romantic mood lighting with the mammogram machine. They should get some music in this room ... that would really set the mood. "Change position, hold, move a little, hold, other boob, hold ... OK, I should have enough views now. Just pop the gown back on while I check the results in the other room."

She didn't disappear for very long though, "The mammogram isn't really showing us anything, so grab your stuff from the change room, I'll take you through to the ultrasound waiting area."

Wow, I couldn't believe the mammogram couldn't see the lump. Not only could I feel the lump very easily, but the nurse had even put this little metallic arrow sticker on my boob so it pointed out the exact location on the films.

"It happens sometimes if the lump is very deep or around on the side of the breast," she explained as she led me to the next waiting room. "It's nothing to worry about, the ultrasound is a lot more accurate."

I guess this nurse wasn't used to someone with my strong attitude, because I actually wasn't worried at all, I was just feeling pained at the fact that I now had to spend more valuable time having more tests. This was seriously beginning to look as if it was turning into an all-day sucker.

The ultrasound waiting room is less a waiting room, and more a corridor with a few seats. It has that feeling of sitting outside the teacher's office. No-one speaks, no-one makes eye contact, and no-one remembered to bring anything to read, because this waiting room doesn't come with any magazines, good or bad ones. So, there I sat, dressed for a 70s garden party, hugging my clothing, and watching the doors to see which would open for me, and hoping I wouldn't be sitting there for too long.

Regardless of what you're getting checked with the ultrasound, whether it's the middle of summer, or how much the radiographer apologises, the gel will undoubtedly cause you to flinch with cold shock the moment it is applied, and the feeling will not subside as the hand scanner squishes and spreads the gel far and wide. Apart from the cold, this special ultrasound gel also has its own unique smell of a non-descript medical odour and has the feeling of slime mixed with beach sand. And irrespective of how well you try to clean up, you will continue to feel the presence of the gel until you finally give in and have the longest, hottest and soapiest shower you feel you can handle.

TAP TAP TAP ... the radiographer moved the hand scanner over my boob, under my arm, up my neck, only stopping to take screen captures and type in labels of what she was seeing. Have you ever noticed they angle the screen just enough so you think you will be able to see what they're looking at when you first sit on the bed? Once you're in position with your body on display, there is the realisation that you can't see anything meaningful without craning your head into an unnatural position.

The hospital where I had my first ultrasound actually had a mirrored monitor hanging from the ceiling, angled in such a way where I could see exactly what the radiographer was looking at. While I was strongly tempted to ask if it was a boy or a girl, a quick glance at the seriousness on the radiographer's face made me rethink my joke. She didn't look like she was in the mood to find anything funny, and I very much doubt it was the first time she had heard someone use this comment in an effort to alleviate the tension in the room.

Just as I began to think my entire upper body was covered in gel, she lifted the handpiece away, wiped it off and closed my gown which immediately stuck to me as if I was in a wet t-shirt contest.

"I'll just need to check with the senior radiologist, to see if he wants any further images. You can clean yourself up for now, I won't be long." With that chipper remark, she bounded from the room leaving me in a dimly lit space on my own, with a box of tissues and no explanation about what she had found.

While tissues are used for all kinds of personal body clean ups, they're not actually designed for any other use than a minor nose blowing. After destroying multiple tissues in my failed clean-up attempt, I decided to take a leaf out of the workshop handbook and use my floral gown as a cleaning rag. The trick is to wipe most of the gel off with the tissues, and then use the outside of the gown to do a final wipe down. That way you don't end up re-applying the wiped off gel as soon as you put the gown back on.

A flash of light from the corridor, announced that my serious radiographer had come back into the room, but this time she had a friend. She had returned with the senior radiologist.

"As you have probably already realized, there is an anomaly in your right breast. I'd like to do a needle biopsy of it for further inspection. I can do that today if you like, or you can make an appointment to come back at a different time if you need to think about it."

Why would I want to think about it? I'd already spent most of my day hanging about in my 70s fancy dress, so we might as well continue and totally write this day off. Besides, when you have to book in for tests you end up spending weeks tossing and turning, thinking about what's going to happen. After the actual test, you spend weeks again tossing and turning, waiting for the results. My answer was and was always going to be "Let's get it sorted today; get it over and done with; then I can go home and get on with what's important."

Had I known what the needle biopsy involved, I'm not sure I would have been so quick to answer. This is not just one of your regular type needles, it's actually 10 times the size of a regular needle, the pointy end resembled a 2B pencil a first grader has been using all day. This unusual tool is housed inside what appeared to be a pressure powered staple gun. You might think I'm exaggerating because of my dislike of needles, but I have never ever seen such a torture device aimed at any part of my body.

Thump ... Thump ... Thump ...

Sure, my boobs aren't all that sensitive. It's pretty common for larger breasts to have less feeling, almost as if the nerve endings are buried way down deep under all that padding. But they were going deep, and while it wasn't the sharp pain of a needle, it still wasn't a walk in the park.

Thump ... Thump ... Thump ...

Wow, how many chunks do they need?

Although this is possibly the best way to retrieve accurate biopsies from a boob, it does leave some major artwork behind. While I didn't see much bruising that night, the following night revealed the yellowing tell-tale marks of bruises starting to show off each individual THUMP. The following days only added several more colours to the palette and then decided to throw in good quality pain over my entire right upper side to accompany the colourful display.

The problem when your boob is sore and bruised is that not only every movement you make causes you to flinch in pain, but the simple act of sleeping can be difficult. I like to sleep on my stomach, hugging my pillow. I discovered very quickly, and painfully, that I would be spending the next week sleeping on my back. Little did I realise this was just the beginning of many painful and sleepless nights to come.

Chapter 3
He's Always Been *MY* Dr Mark.

I should preface this by saying there really is never a good way or time to receive bad news. Even if deep down in your gut you already have an idea the news isn't going to be great, you can never truly prepare yourself fully for that confirmation. The other thing you should not do is look at a doctor's report, especially if you don't have a medical degree.

Sitting at the dining room table with a vegemite sandwich, I kept staring at the envelope containing the radiologists report addressed to Dr Mark. Even though I knew I wouldn't be able to understand it, I still could not contain my curiosity. Hey, I'm a smart girl, there might be something in the report that I can figure out, so I carefully opened it and took out the letter. I wasn't wrong, it was full of technical, medical jargon, written only for a doctor's eyes. Re-reading it over my sandwich did not help it make any more sense. It did, however, deepen the feeling of foreboding.

Foreboding is not nearly a big enough, or descriptive enough word for the feeling I felt when Dr Mark, my GP of over 24 years rang me, himself, not his receptionist, to arrange an appointment.

"I've received your biopsy results, and I'd really like to see you as soon as possible."

Wow, the marvels of the digital age. He didn't need the report that was sitting on my dining room table, he already had this information.

"Yep, all good," I replied with a fake cheerfulness, hoping he wouldn't notice that I had started to tremble with … what was that … fear?

"I have an appointment with you for Friday afternoon."

"No, Andrea," Dr Mark sounded pretty serious, and using my full name instead of Andy, was starting to worry me deep down inside. "I can fit you in at 3 o'clock this afternoon, and you might want to bring Mick with you," Dr Mark left it at that. He didn't give me any further information, or maybe he did and I just tuned out. I don't even remember hanging up the phone.

On the surface it was a seemingly normal request, but I immediately started to shake uncontrollably, and then I caught myself, half an hour later, standing in the kitchen with a well boiled kettle, just staring out the window in a total daze. I'm sure everyone's brain short circuits and goes on holiday when subjected to overwhelming information. Mine is particularly good at this and does not even send a postcard to say where it's gone. There were no thoughts involved, just a total blank.

At the medical centre, later that day, I was only semi distracted by Mick.

Mick is worse than your average kid when being asked to sit quietly on any given situation but put him on a row of plastic chairs in the local doctor's waiting room, and his hyperactive nervous leg jiggle gets going.

Mick only has two forms of waiting; he either paces up and down in the carpark and smokes or sits and jiggles, shaking the entire row of conjoined plastic seats in the process.

"Mick, quit it!" I scowled at him while we waited for the doctor.

"Wha?" he responded, not aware of his nervous twitching.

"Never mind," I said, presuming the other patients could always move if they didn't like it. I went back to playing my little head games in the waiting room.

When I'm not in the mood to or can't focus my brain enough to read gossip magazines, I like to people watch and play little games in my head about which person is the sick one, and what they're here for. It's not an overly complicated game, but I did say that it's my backup for when I can't concentrate on the gossip columns.

Instinct pulled me out of my brain game and told me to look past reception towards the doctor's rooms, just in time to see Dr Mark, face drawn and serious, coming toward me. I've never seen him look so serious. He offered no smiles, small talk, or even a "how are you". I looked at Mick and he had the same serious look on his face, or was it fear?

My mind was off again on an unscheduled holiday. Dr Mark had finally used that word ... Cancer. And then some time after that my brain had short circuited again.

But Mick and Dr Mark were still talking. 'What were they saying? ... When did I stop hearing the words?'

"Now I need to get you into hospital as quickly as possible. Do you have a preference of hospital?" Dr Mark was looking directly at me, not realizing I had not been listening. "Charlie's, if we can. We don't have private insurance, so it'll have to be public."

But even as I said the words, I felt it was not me speaking. It was like I was eavesdropping on a conversation in the next room. There was the noise of someone speaking but no distinguishable words. I was feeling confused. Is this what they call an out of body experience? What was happening?

I stared at the doctor; then at Mick. Their mouths were moving. They were talking about me, but it was just white noise. Dr Mark looked at me, but he did not smile reassuringly, as he usually does, nor did he try to include me in the conversation. He must have realised I'd shut down. He must have seen I couldn't be part of the conversation at this time. He continued talking to Mick, making phone calls and typing on his computer. I just sat. I just stared. I just waited. There were no thoughts. There were no feelings. There was no understanding. There was a total void.

If you receive any word from my brain, please send it home with an assurance that it is loved and missed, and I'm very sorry for everything it's been through.

Chapter 4
Start Spreading the News

(to the tune of New York New York)

Start spreading the news ... I'm sharing today.
I want to share no part of it, you heard, you heard.
These regular boobs, are wanting to stay.
I'm right here in the thick of it, you heard, you heard.
I wanna wake up, and then see it was all a dream.
And find out, it's not as bad as it all seems.
This horrible news is spreading your way.
I'll fight my way through it, you heard, you heard.
If I can make it through,
I'll make it with you.
I'll fight my way through, you heard, you heard.

Thankfully Mick was the one who drove home, after receiving the news from Dr Mark, since I was still trying to comprehend it all. With my brain working on overdrive,

I wasn't capable of holding a meaningful conversation let alone being able to drive a vehicle and pay attention to the road.

Since the news hadn't really sunk in, Mick decided to take a quick detour past his Dad's house to pick up the chainsaw ready for the weekend of garden destruction.

"Do you think we should tell him?" I asked Mick, unsure if I was ready to share what didn't yet seem real, let alone know how to share this kind of news to one of the few people who probably knew me better than I know myself.

"We have to," Mick answered, as we pulled into his Dad's driveway. "He knows you too well, he'll see there is something wrong."

"Willkommen in unserem Zuhause," was the greeting along with hugs and kisses as we headed directly for the heart of Fred's house – it's what we had done for the past fifteen or so years. Mick's Dad was a pastry chef and baker, and his Mum (since passed) was a German Chef, so the heart of their home was the warm, welcoming and often yummy smelling kitchen.

"What's wrong," Fred looked at me. "Son?" and then gave Mick a worried and serious look.

"We've just come from the doctor," Mick said calmly. "Andy has breast cancer." Yep, he just spat it out quick. Rip that band aid off. It's going to do the same damage whether you go fast or slow, so it's better to just dive in and get that pain over with quickly.

"Oh Geeez." Fred was visibly shocked. "You'll be fine."

His words were positive, but his body language gave away how devastating this news was. In typical father and son style, Mick and Fred avoided the emotion of the situation by changing the subject as quickly as Mick had introduced it, leaving me to sit with my own thoughts and wonder if this was actually some kind of alternative reality. If you've read any sci-fi or fantasy books, you'd realise that time flows totally differently in alternative realities. There's no rules. One moment it's morning and you're busy getting your work done, then the next moment you're sitting on the back patio, watching the sun going down and wondering what happened to make your life change so dramatically in just a few hours.

I knew I had other important people to share this still seemingly unrealistic news with as soon as possible, but I really wasn't sure how to get started. It's not like you can just ring and blurt it all out, and I certainly wasn't up to driving all over town. Besides, the quick, blurt it out approach might have worked with Mick's Dad, but I didn't think it was quite the right approach for my Mum and Dad, or my sister. I was going to have to do this myself and with a little more tact.

Mick put a stiff scotch and soda in front of me, causing me to change the direction of my gaze but not the location of my mind. "So, what are we going to do?" he asked quietly. I hadn't even started thinking about the future or what we were going to do. My mind was only just starting to come out of its comatose state and allow me to digest this life changing news we'd received; although, I guess it was just something for him to say to get the conversation started.

Mick is one for having plans. He is always adamant about

needing to know when and where well ahead of any situation so he can prepare himself mentally. Absolutely everything needs to be entered onto the calendar hanging in the kitchen. This was not going to be easy for him. It wasn't like the race car where he could get out his tools and just fix it, or a weed in the garden, he could just pull out.

"About...?" I looked at him as though from a distance, even though he was seated right next to me. What a stupid thing to say. I knew darn well what about. Somehow it just didn't seem real. What was I waiting for? Someone to tell me it was a stupid and heartless joke? Did I think that by sitting here staring at the sun going down it would make everything clearer, or better still, it would all just magically go away? Suddenly I was a grown up with grown up problems and I didn't want to be. I wanted to be a kid where my parents would fix it all for me.

My parents. I sighed, "I guess I'd better make a couple of calls."

I turned and picked up the landline phone from its cradle behind me. This magical device which invited me into this world of horror, I was in turn, going to use to invite others along for the ride. I thumbed the speed dial arrows until I reached Mum and Dad's phone number - supposing that would be the easier one ...

I was not sure what I was going to say. If it still didn't feel real to me, how was I going to tell someone else? If I didn't tell them now, when would be the right time to share this news? Just like a band aid ... short, sharp, quick action; cause the same level of pain, but don't drag it out.

"Hi Mum, ummmmmmm...." Was I stalling? or just not sure how to start? "There's no easy way to say this... I have some really crappy news. I've just found out I have Breast Cancer ..."

Oh Crap…

there it is.

I said it out loud.

I guess that made it real.

My mind was dragged back from its reality holiday with a sharp tug. I would not be expecting postcards. I snapped back to reality with such sudden clarity and awareness realising this was not a dream. This was not happening in a book. This was not happening to someone else. It was actually happening to me. This was my new reality and I had to face it as the grownup I was.

"I HAVE CANCER …"

I listened to my Mum take a deep shaky breath, and could hear Dad coming closer to the speakerphone, his feet shuffling on their wooden floor. They always use the speakerphone, which normally I don't like, but this time it was definitely going to make my announcement easier by telling them both at the same time. I didn't think I'd be able to repeat myself, and judging by Mum's voice, I didn't think she was ready to repeat the news to Dad. But it still didn't feel right to do this over the phone, even if I did have to let them know as quickly as possible. It felt too impersonal.

"Mum?" I plucked up some courage from deep within,

needing to break the silence and at the same time needing to give her the details to help make it more real for her. If I'd left it as just that statement she would wonder later if it was real. There would be nothing to hang onto. So, I shared, but quickly, so I would leave no room for her to interrupt with questions. One thing I did know was that I could not deal with questions right now.

"I went to see Dr Mark last week about a lump I found in my breast. He sent me for a mammogram which turned into an ultrasound and then a biopsy. Dr Mark called me this afternoon and told me to bring Mick. I knew there was something wrong when he called, because a doctor doesn't normally ring you at home, does he? Mick came home from work early so he could go with me, which was good because I don't know how much I took in. The doctor is trying to get me into hospital as quickly as possible so they can work out what to do....." I gulped in a huge gasp of air ....

"Oh sweetheart. You're sure then?" Mum asked, but Dad was silent in the background. Although I couldn't hear him, I knew he was still there, listening. I could see him in my mind just standing there with a troubled and confused look on his face, barely comprehending the reality of what he had just heard. I am so much like my Dad in some ways. The shock sets in and we just outwardly shut down until the brain can fully process the news. Mum is different, she seems to process this kind of news quickly and had the right response at the ready.

"Honey, you know that your Dad and I are here for you, whatever you need. You will be strong and get through this ... and we will be there for you ..."

I don't know if it was Mum's strong voice, the thought of Dad in the background or that finally reality had hit home. The tears started pouring down my eyes. I felt my face screwing up and I started bawling like a baby. I couldn't control it. There was no warning. The floodgates had opened.

I couldn't listen anymore, and I most certainly couldn't speak, so I held the phone out to Mick who handed me the tissue box at the same time. I guess it had to happen. The tears had to start at some point. Mum was just being so calm and so nice and so loving. In between the silent sobs, I listened to Mick talk to Mum on the phone.

"I'm sorry Maria," Mick was saying "It's finally sunk in, and she's broken down. She might be able to talk again later. .... aha ..... yeah I know you are .... I will .... " I didn't have to hear the other side of the conversation to know that Mum was still saying that they would be there for me, for us, if there was anything we needed and for Mick to take care of me.

The tears kept coming. I couldn't control it. Each time I thought I had it under control, the tears would well up again. I sat at the table with my head in my hands and let the sobs continue, not remembering how long it had been since I'd cried this hard. If ever. Mick just watched me with his loving eyes and waited patiently until I was able to start talking again.

"I'm sorry, I'm being such a baby. I don't know what's happening to me..." I sniffled through the drying tears. After what felt like an hour of blubbering, but I'm sure it was only a few minutes, I managed to contribute to the conversation again.

"You're not being a baby," Mick put his hand on my arm for reassurance. "You've had a big shock, and it's finally setting in. Don't try to control it, just let go."

"It's been a big shock for you too," I blubbered "I don't see you acting like a big girl."

"No, but I may go and have a shower later ..." he left the sentence hanging. I knew what he meant. Mick wasn't insensitive, but he was raised to be that strong 'boys don't cry in public' type, especially when they're being strong for their girl.

I guess we were going to learn how to deal with this together. It's not as if either of us had any knowledge or experience with cancer, but with Mick's history of medical exploits - ankle reconstruction, multiple eye surgeries and finally slipping in the shower and impaling his arm - we were pretty experienced with supporting each other through some tough times.

I sighed and picked up the phone again, "I'd better ring Fran."

"Are you sure calling your sister is such a good idea?" Mick had concern written all over his face. "It can wait until tomorrow."

"I owe it to her before Mum decides to call her. She has to hear it from me. Just be on the ready if I break down again." I hit the speed dial for my sister's phone number.

"Hi chick, how are you doing?" I said when my little sister answered the phone. Although there's eight years between us, we're pretty close, and getting closer as we get older. We are so different in many ways; both in appearance and personality. Fran is a free spirited, social butterfly who loves being a Mum and who has never been happy sitting in one place too long. I have so many different entries for phone numbers and addresses in my book for her, but at least for the last few years she's been living locally, allowing us to get to know each other as grown women.

"Honey," I figured I would try to make it quick as there was no way to sugar coat this type of news. "There's no easy way to say this. I have just been told I have Breast Cancer." Oh Crap, I could hear the tears on the other end of the phone, but I could also hear her trying to hide them from me.

"When, uh how....? oh shit ....." she stumbled through the words. I could picture the confusion, shock and sadness all rolled into one big emotion on the other end of the phone. I could feel my own tears trying to make a break for it, but I was refusing to give in. If I grabbed a tissue, it would be giving in. So I held back. But at the same time decided that details could wait until we caught up face to face.

Mick made me a fresh drink and we spent the next hour or so crying, talking and trying to make sense of what had happened today, before heading off to bed for a sleepless night. The amount of alcohol consumed should have ensured me a dreamless coma, but unfortunately some information just can't be drowned out. We both tossed and turned all night, only to wake up much too early with sore heads and red eyes and cotton wool mouths.

Telling family the news was always going to be difficult.

I'm afraid I chickened out when it came to letting the rest of our family and friends know, leaving them to find out through the gossip vine or allowing Mick to break the news. The weekend busy bee turned out to be the most opportune time to inform many of our friends, allowing them to be energised by their emotions.

While telling my business partner, Suze, only a couple of weeks after her own sister had been diagnosed, was a very difficult task, there was one person I kept putting off calling. I assumed the longer I waited, the more likely it was that I would find the right way to share the news. Or maybe I thought it would just go away and I wouldn't have to tell her anything.

But on the evening of our busy bee, my best friend Sue rang me out of the blue ... and it really was the hardest phone call of all. I took the phone to the bedroom, away from the hard workers who had stayed on for a few ales, shut the door and quietly broke the news to her. At first, she wasn't sure if she'd heard me correctly. Then I heard the tears start and the conversation died.

"Mum, what's wrong?" I heard my 9-year-old goddaughter, Lucy in the background, but Sue couldn't find the words to explain.

"I'll ring you back when we can talk," I sobbed down the phone and hung up knowing that Sue's husband, Paul, and daughter would be comforting her. I really didn't want to tell her like this. This was one time I didn't want my best friend to be living over 3000km away in the little north west town of Paraburdoo. I wanted my best friend to be sitting on the bed with me. I wanted to hug her and be hugged back and to share our tears. I wanted to scream with her that it wasn't fair. I wanted her to look at me and tell me without words that we would get through this together. But instead I sat on the bed alone, and cried silently, until I could face the friends who had been working in our garden all day.

Chapter 5
Waiting to Meet the Team

Once you've come to terms with the fact that you actually have cancer, all you want to do is move onto the next stage and get rid of it. Well that's the way Mick and I thought about it anyway.

This is the problem, there is a solution, let's get moving and fix it.

But unfortunately, the length of time from that moment of being diagnosed to beginning the treatment can seem like an absolute age, chocked full of tests, scans, biopsies and doctor reports. And that's not all the waiting you have to do throughout the entire journey. I'll be the first to admit that I'm not the most patient person in the world, especially when it's related to something I personally want or need. I was, am and will probably always be that person who shakes, pokes and minutely examines each Christmas present under the tree, and even though I might be in my 40s, I will still wake up at the crack of dawn on Christmas morning preferring unwrapping gifts to eating breakfast. This experience only proved I am not cut out to wait for anything.

In the beginning, Dr Mark had to get me into the public hospital system as quickly as possible, which eventuated in several letters, some even from the same hospitals, arriving in my mailbox. It was like I was suddenly the most popular kid being invited to everyone's birthday party, only I knew I would only be able to attend just the one.

"Dr Mark," I rang him to check which appointment letter I needed to pay attention to. "Which one of these appointments is the right one?"

"None," he replied. "I need to get you in much quicker than that.

I'll ring you when I have an appointment I'm happy with."

Hey, I love having a doctor with dedication, but his response wasn't doing anything for my nervousness. I resigned myself to the fact that nothing would be done for several weeks and tried to distract myself with the job of making money designing marketing fliers that no-one wants to read.

It wasn't that long though, (if you can call a few days of jumping every time the phone rang, a short length of time), before Dr Mark got back to me with the winning date. "I have an appointment for you at the Breast Clinic in Charlies for next Tuesday." He seemed so proud of all the hard work he had done to push me through the public hospital queue so quickly.

"*Next* Tuesday?" Mick spluttered out his beer when I told him the news that night.

The wait was over, and it was suddenly all about to happen, and in less than a week. I know we had been waiting for this moment, but I don't think once we had the actual date, we were fully prepared for what was about to happen. Would I be going in for surgery? Would I be starting chemo straight away? Should I pack an overnight bag for the appointment, just in case? Should I email my clients and warn them I might be out of action for a little while?

What's that saying about assuming? There was no discussion of treatment, no booking in for surgery. This was a chance to meet the team and start the process all over again right from the beginning.

We found out quickly that specialist departments don't like to trust the results of anyone else and will book you in for all the same tests all over again. Then book you in to go over the reports again, and then finally book you in to make a choice about what you would like to do, as if you're renovating a house and you need to choose the right tiles to go with the cabinets.

While it's all a very thorough process full of checks and balances, from the moment of introduction to your cancerous growth, all you really want to do is evict the unwelcome guest from your breast. Meeting the "team" who will be assisting you on your journey, is not high on the priority list.

One of the people in your personal team is your very own breast care nurse. She comes into each appointment with you, helps you understand all the terminology, helps you book other appointments, and she even gives you a direct phone number so that when you get home and think "what did that mean again?", you can ring and ask her.

Following our first appointment at the Breast Clinic in Charlies, nurse Sholeh ushered Mick and me into a private room with a nice overstuffed couch, mood lighting, and if I'm not mistaken there was even scented candles flickering away in the corner. Mick gave me the kind of terrified "get me out of here" look that pretty much any very typical Aussie male would give in this situation.

"Just go with it and we'll see what she wants," I whispered to Mick. Slightly wary of the whole situation myself.

"Take a seat and make yourself comfortable," nurse Sholeh breathed out in her soft airy voice as she sat across the brochure laden coffee table from us. "So," she looked directly at Mick with a gentle smile and the kindest eyes, "how are you feeeeeeeeling."

I honestly thought I was going to laugh out loud right there, just looking at Mick's face. Even now, every time we look back at that situation it makes us laugh. Poor nurse Sholeh had no idea that we are the type of people who were more comfortable chatting over a few drinks with a close friend rather than over some scented candles with a total stranger.

We did try to be as polite as possible, while attempting to wrap the meeting up quickly.

I guess nurse Sholeh worked out we needed a different approach, so the following appointment we were introduced to our new Breast Care nurse, Liz. She didn't ask Mick to share his feelings, and for that he is still grateful.

Armed with a load of appointments for the next week, I realised how lucky I am to be working for myself. It meant I could head off for any number of scans, biopsies and general medical people meet and greets throughout the week and not have to be worried about upsetting the boss with the amount of time I needed to take off work. It also meant I could take a moment to catch up with friends in between appointments.

"I have a high contrast scan today," I had rung my business partner, Suze. "Do you want to catch up for a late lunch when I get out?"

"Sounds like a plan," she replied. "How about I meet you at the Balmoral?" It was an easy drive there from the city, and it was a close walk from Suze's home-office, so it was the perfect choice of location, and one that we'd taken advantage of for 'business meetings' a few times.

"Perfect," I cheered, "I'll text you when I'm on my way. See you there."

While I'm pretty sure I'd been signed up to test out all the big donut shaped scanning machines in the hospital prior to surgery, this one actually required me to be injected with a radioactive dye first.

"It's so all the nasties will glow in the dark, just like the bright yellow tracksuit we give you to wear," the nurse explained with a little joke. I could just imagine my body glowing as brightly as my tracksuit as the radioactive dye travelled through my veins, lighting up sections of 'bad boy parties' for the medical team to investigate more closely. Little did I realise, that by the end of the day and for the next week, the outside of my body would also be glowing like a red ember direct from the fireplace.

"You look flushed," Suze commented as we grabbed a table in the beer garden after my scans were complete, and I'd changed back into some clothing that was less 70's lounging attire. What is it with hospitals and 70s fancy dress? And what did they make people wear in the 70s anyway?

"I've just been running around," I said. I was feeling a little prickly with heat, but it wasn't exactly a cool day, and the stress of so many hospital appointments over the past week, and still no plan in sight was also getting to me.

"So I would recommend a nice cold beer then." Suze grinned a cheeky grin at the thought of having a drink in the middle of the day, in the middle of the week.
"I couldn't agree more," I replied. "We're such a bad influence on each other."

But as the beer glasses and empty lunch plates were cleared away, and our conversation about work was reaching the point that we should probably get back to it, Suze commented again.

"You really are looking very red."

I had to agree, I wasn't just feeling prickly anymore, this was starting to feel very uncomfortable. I was now feeling flushed and very itchy all over, and a simple splash of water from the ladies' room wasn't helping in the slightest.

It was no longer just my face feeling prickly and flushed, my head was now itchy, my armpits were itchy, inside my ears were itchy, my eyeballs were itchy, even my tongue was itchy.

Rushing through the front door on arriving home, I said a quick hello to the dogs and stripped off every stitch of clothing while running to the bathroom, and then jumped straight under a full pressure, cold shower. Oh boy that felt good. But sitting on the floor of the shower, I immediately noticed a major problem.

While I was under the water, the itchiness and burning subsided due to little rain drops of coldness caressing my burning skin, but the second I stepped out my burning skin immediately dried, and the itching immediately resumed, this time with a vengeance.

There was no choice. I would have to 'man up', and drive the half hour to the other side of town to visit Dr Mark for a prescription for some of that really good Cortisone cream, as this was looking like a situation where the teeny tubes of the lightweight stuff you get over the counter from the chemist, was not going to cut the mustard.

That evening, Mick's rough workshop hands were like a gentle loofah, adding thick lashings of cream to the parts of my body that I couldn't reach. I was like strawberries and cream - heavy on the cream please.

By the end of a week of applying cream to my hives, Mick commented, "I'm going to have to start wearing gloves at work now, because my hands are all soft and delicate."

So now when I go to the hospital, I am part of the red

crowd. Red dots and allergy warning labels on every piece of medical paperwork, a red hat in surgery, and red ID band on my wrist and ankle. No IV Iodine allowed for this body.

Chapter 6
You Can't Control it with Stubborn

D day was finally here, or should I call it Double D day since it was all about the boobs. This was about to be an experience beyond anything I had ever imagined, since it was my first time in surgery. I hadn't even broken a bone before, and if you know how many times I'd been in motorbike and car accidents, you will understand how much of a major achievement that actually is.

Our arrival at the hospital ground floor was a blur of checking in, waiting around, answering questions, completing paperwork, and more waiting. Following the completion of all the forms, we were sent to the second floor waiting room, which was smaller but at least here I could see the same look of apprehension on the faces around us. To say I was nervous and scared at the same time would have been a slight understatement.

Everyone was waiting, with grumbling, empty stomachs, to be directed to change into the attractive surgery gown with the gaping back and some chux undies before being upgraded to the third waiting room. The third and final section of waiting for surgery comes with your very own bed.

"Andrea?" a nurse broke me out of my wandering thoughts about a nice strong coffee. She beckoned me to follow, handed me a gown, and pointed me in the direction of the change rooms. "You have showered with the pre-wash?" she asked.

"Yes" I replied. I felt the butterflies flutter nervously in my empty stomach. Suddenly this felt very real.

I sighed and went into the small cubicle to get changed. "Undies too love," called the nurse. It's my boob they're operating on, why no undies? Ah well. What do I know, so I did as I was told.

Once changed into the adorable ensemble of baby blue open back gown, chux undies, knee high white stockings with peek-a-boo toes and a cute pink allergy alert shower cap, the nurse settled me into one of the beds. Mick came through into the huge and busy ward, led by another nurse as she proceeded to attach red name tags to my wrist and ankle.

"How are you feeling?" he asked. What did he want to hear me say? 'Nervous? Scared? Downright Terrified?'

"OK I guess..." although as I said it, I could hear in the tone of my own voice that it wasn't really an accurate description of how I was feeling.

"They made me wear the chux undies" I complained, and

Mick laughed. He'd been through this a few times before and knew all about them. I guess they would be even more embarrassing for a bloke to wear, as they don't have any elastic. He grabbed all my clothes and packed them into my overnight bag, and then just sat silently with me as we watched all the other people waiting for their surgery. Some alone, some with family, but all quiet in their own thoughts. I like to people watch, playing little stories over in my head and wondering how accurate I am.

"OK Luv, it's your turn." A cheerful nurse and orderly were at my side. "I'll need your glasses," she said, and took them from me, placing them into a kidney dish. Without my glasses the world turns into an indecipherable blur, so I've rarely been seen without them since discovering I was severely short sighted at the age of sixteen. How I'd managed to make it through school and actually compete in squash tournaments without them for so long is anyone's guess. Now if they're not on my face, they are within easy reach.

Amid the hustle and bustle I heard Mick say, "I'll see you on the other side." He kissed me and smiled some confidence at me, as if he was trying to transmit some positive force.

It was time to lay back and stare at the blurry ceiling. I did try to follow where we were going but as the orderly pushed me through one corridor after another, sneaking around the back alleys to the operating theatre, I lost track. I couldn't see much anyway, but closing my eyes was definitely not an option. That would just cause me to feel car sick and going into surgery feeling crook was probably not the best idea. So, I decided to stick with it and distract my nervousness by trying to make sense of the blurry shapes along the way.

Bang ... bang, the foot of my bed crashed open two doors, just like in the movies. But this was one very small room, very unlike the movies. It was more like a walk-in-wardrobe, wall to wall cupboards and shelving with just enough room for people to walk on each side of the bed. I really thought an operating theatre would be heaps bigger than this. I watched as fuzzy ghost like shapes moved about the room, opened packets, stuck patches on various parts of my body, applied the blood pressure arm band, and then tried to get the needle in my vein.

"Do you normally have a problem with your veins?" the Anaesthetist asked.

"I've never had surgery before," I responded to the blurry figure tapping my arm, looking for a vein.

"I will have to use a child's needle to get you started," he said. "Your veins look good on the surface, but they're actually very small and wriggly."

I started to wonder how they could possibly do an operation in such a small room with so many people in it. Even though they were all ghostly shapes, I could work out that there were at least 10 people fussing about me in a room the size of my bathroom.

thump thump thump thump

I could hear my heartbeat speeding up, and my breathing was speeding up to a pant, trying to keep time.

"Calm down. Breathe deep. Calm down." I silently told

myself, trying to control my breathing. "Settle. It'll be OK. Oh crap. I'm losing it. I can't control my breathing. I think I'm going to hyperventilate."

The harder I tried, the worse it got. I could feel my breath shaking as I exhaled, and before long I was in full scale panic mode.

Tears flooded my eyes causing my already blurry world to disappear totally under water, my heartbeat drummed too loudly in my ears, my stomach started to squirm reminding me that the only contents were stomach acid and my breathing imitated an asthmatic.

I wanted to wipe my eyes, I wanted to roll over and bury my face in my pillow. I wanted to just get up and run away. But instead I just lay still, shaking and terrified, quietly wishing it was all over.

Someone gently took my hand, and a soft female voice spoke to me calmly. I don't remember what she said, I just remember hearing the sound of her voice and feeling immediately calmer.

Someone else, at the foot of my bed told a funny story which I no longer remember but know I couldn't help but laugh at the time. The blurry people had all stopped fussing over me, and before I knew it, I was smiling and laughing through my tears. I could feel my breathing calm down, and my heartbeat came back to an almost normal beat.

Bang bang, I was on the move again as the foot of my bed crashed open two more doors into a much bigger room. From what I could work out, through my fuzzy, still slightly underwater eyesight, this was more like the room you saw in the movies. Big overhead lights, more people, lots of beeping machines and music, not loud, but it was there in the background.

"Just shuffle your bum over to this bed," I tried to do as I was told.

"Hey, Dr Yeo said you're a drag racer. Is that true?" the disembodied voice came from behind me.

"Not yet, but as soon as I kick this cancer I will be." I smiled at the thought that it wouldn't be long before I would be sitting behind the wheel of my bright green Torana.

But still no matter how much I tried to think of the good and how hard I tried to fight it; I could feel that panic starting to build inside me again.

"That's pretty cool. Now, you're just going to feel some cold in your armmmmm ...."

* * * * *

"Andrea, are you with us?" I could hear people talking. Everything was bright, but I couldn't open my eyes. I felt heavy ... oh dear god ... THE PAIN .... hell, that hurt. That was beyond any pain I had ever known. What were they doing to me? Had I woken up in the middle of surgery? This couldn't be right. No-one told me I would be feeling pain like this.

"Andrea, are you in pain? From 1 to 10 how bad is the

pain" I heard a voice at my side.

I could hear someone screaming. Someone was screaming in pain. Couldn't they stop that person screaming? ...

oh ... that was me screaming. "yes... yes, pain" I screamed. I couldn't work out where the pain was, but my whole body was screaming to make it stop. Even the action of opening my eyes to the bright light of the post-surgery recovery room made the pain more intense.

Then, almost as suddenly as I had felt the pain, ahhhhh, it went away, followed by the bright ward and the nurses around my bed. I didn't mind. "Bye bye world. Perhaps I've died," I thought to myself. It didn't matter, as long as I didn't feel that pain anymore.

I had always thought that the level of pain you could handle was relative to how much you allow it to affect you. But I have since found out that there is a level of pain that transcends beyond what you can control with pure stubbornness. When it comes to dealing with pain, I am a pretty stubborn person with an extremely high tolerance.

I woke up again to find I had not died, but instead found myself in a dark hospital room, surrounded by soft pillows. I also discovered, very quickly, that even turning my head slightly brought my mind back to the reality that I've just had my lymph nodes scooped out of my armpit like an ice-cream and the cancer cut out of my boob. And just like the rude awakening of the pain senses, my bladder had woken, and was being extremely persistent about attracting my attention.

How was I going to manage this? I tried to sit up, but the

pain was too intense, I tried to roll sideways instead of pushing myself up into a sitting position, but still the pain was beyond anything even my own stubbornness could handle. And yet, under all that pain, my bladder was screaming that if I didn't do something quickly, I would soon be lying in a warm wet bed.

"Easy does it," a nurse quietly but forcefully pushed me back down on the pillow.

"But I need to pee," I screwed my face up showing that it was an immediate need.

"OK, let's see if you can walk, but we'll take if very gently." She pushed the remote button on the bed which slowly eased me into a sitting position without causing too much pain. "How does that feel so far?"

"That's ok," I responded. My bladder had settled down a little, obviously realising that I was doing what I could to help it out as long as it was patient.

"Now gently swing your legs over the edge and I'll help you up. We only need to shuffle across the room."

What I didn't realise until that moment is that I had quite a few tubes attached which had to accompany me on my journey, and any sudden movement I made caused knee buckling pain. So, the nurse and I made very slow gentle progress to the toilet only a couple of meters away, and then after much relief, an equally slow return journey. Then I fell into pain induced exhausted sleep.

I had never been in a situation where I needed someone to help me do the basics, like help me out of bed, shower, change clothes and even go to the toilet. I had experienced pain before, but nothing like this.

In my short stay on the day ward, the nurses seemed to constantly fuss about me, writing things down, asking questions, taking my pulse, taking my blood pressure, checking dressings and drains. Someone even came to tell me about the exercises I would have to do to make sure I kept good movement in my arms. I just quietly closed my eyes and wished them all to Hell. I didn't want to move, I didn't want to learn exercises, I didn't want a cup of tea or a ham sandwich, I just wanted to sleep.

AND, I wanted to go home.

****

"Sorry babe, I'm trying to be careful" Mick glanced across at me in the car, with concern written all over his face. It was only the day after surgery, and I wasn't on nearly enough painkillers to cope with the drive home.

"I know," I whispered back, whispering because simply the act of talking would cause pain and the whole process of getting dressed and walking across the hospital car park had already brought me to the absolute brink of what pain I was able to cope with.

So why are there speed bumps in hospital car parks? And do you think the Main Roads department would appreciate a list of all the potholes in the road between the hospital and my house?

Arriving home sent a wave of relief through my body, just knowing that very soon I would be able to be totally still. As I gently made the excruciatingly long trek from the driveway to the lounge bed Mick had carefully set up for me, Mick rushed ahead and temporarily locked the dogs outside, so they didn't jump on me excitedly. Awww, he'd even bought me one of those invalid pillows with the arms. Oh wow, it was so soft and so comfy, and I was so tired. The pain of the last hour of travelling had totally exhausted me.

"Honey... " I heard Mick in the distance.

I thought as I started drifting off, 'I should say something… Yeh. I should… say something …'

One thing that is difficult when you're in a high level of pain is simply sleeping, and yet it's the one thing you crave above anything else. Although I'd prepared the spare room with lots of pillows and the radio tuned into ABC talk back, I found it wasn't simply a case of getting used to sleeping on my back so as not to squash my newly sliced up boob. It was also doing my best not to get tangled up in the drainage tube running from my armpit to an extremely unattractive bottle in its homemade floral, yes you guessed it, 70s style carry bag, sitting on the floor next to my bed.

But the body will always find a way to cope, even if it means sleeping for an hour at a time. That night I managed a heavy, dreamless sleep where I simply felt no pain. Unless I moved, that was.

I woke up, rearranged the pillows so I couldn't roll over, and listened to the type of people who rang a radio station at 2am. I could hear Mick stir in the other room and hoped he would get some sleep instead of lying awake worrying about me. I took some more painkillers and drifted back into that heavy dreamless sleep with the hope that by morning I would begin to feel better.

Chapter 7
I Think I Sprung a Leak

The most bizarre thing about having your lymph nodes and part of your breast removed, is the fact that you wake up with a 3 meter long drainage tube attached to a vacuum bottle that looks like an alien from Mars with its little rubber antenna crossed over in a cute little hug. I'm sure I must have been living under a rock somewhere, because never have I seen this type of contraption attached to a person before. Sure, I've seen similar devices attached to race cars as overflow bottles, but for the next couple of weeks, I was going to be carrying around my own 600ml overflow bottle. Little did I realise at the time that this was nothing compared to the 4 bottles I would have to contend with later in my treatment.

"How am I going to carry this out of the hospital? It'll totally gross everyone out," I asked the nurse, while waiting to be discharged after my first surgery. While I thought that looking at this clear bottle and tube of red fluid being drained from my body into it was very disturbing, I knew there was really only one person in my life who would get a perverse kick out of the idea, and she would snub me forever if I didn't share this particular level of grossness with her.

"You sooooooo have to send me a photo," Sue cooed over the phone when I described this bottle and it's red fluid and floaty bits.

"You've got to be kidding me, surely this is even beyond you," I retorted, although this was one chick who had described her bowel movements to me in absolute detail during her pregnancy.

"No way," she actually sounded eager, "I want to see. I so wish I was there right now." Most friends would say that because they wanted to be there to support their bestie, but not Sue. It's not like she wasn't a supportive friend, she just honestly felt she was missing out on all the cool gory bits. So, I did what only a best friend does in that situation, I sent her photos. Lots of photos showing the line, and the bottle, and all the floaty bits, along with bandage and wound photos.

"I have a leaving gift for you Andrea," the nurse responded to my concern about carting this bottle around for the next couple of weeks. She handed me a mini primary school library book bag, made from someone's kindly donated 70's floral kitchen curtains, only it wasn't for holding any books. My new fashion accessory was going to be the perfect accompaniment to my flannel shirt, tracksuit pants and bottle of floaty bits of me for the next few weeks.

"Some of the lovely ladies at Solaris Care make these bags specifically for your situation," she smiled as she hid my new attachment away in my latest fashion accessory and motioned for me to take it for a little walk to try it out.

"oooo, very nice," I did a gentle little catwalk wiggle and twirl so as not to aggravate the pain from surgery. "I can see this taking off on the streets of Paris."

While I didn't do my usual trick of researching the bottle in great detail, my understanding from the Silver Chain nurses who visited me at home each day to check my dressings, is that the overflow bottle works as a vacuum to remove any additional fluid build-up around the wound area, until the internal wound starts to heal over. What they didn't tell me is that it actually starts to grow over the additional tubing inside, or how much actual tubing there really is on the inside, so when it comes time to remove the tubing, well … let's just say it's an experience like no other.

Are you a quick or slow band aid ripper? Or do you totally chicken out and wait until it falls off in the shower. I'm a quick band aid ripper. I prefer to avoid extending the time the pain lasts for, instead opting for the slightly increased pain level over a much shorter time frame. Just rip it off!!! Then jump around going 'ow ow ow ow' under my breath.

But you can't do this when removing the drainage tubes. I have it under good authority that it needs to be gentle, slow and methodical. Oh, and by the way, there's like another 3 meters of tube inside too. But that experience was yet to come. For now, I was blissfully unaware of the removal process or of the fact that there was more than just

1 or 2 cm hanging about inside me. I was totally focused on the red fluid and floaty bits collecting in my overflow bottle, and measuring its progress each day, looking forward to there being so little drained that I would be free of my encumbrance.

"You'll need a new bottle today," the home visit Silver Chain nurse advised me about a week into my recovery. Wow, I could feel my shoulder smiling already with the prospect of switching the full bottle of floaties for a fresh light weight empty bottle. Clamp, snip, pop the old one in a brown paper bag, and it's done.

"That was quick and easy," I commented.

"You'll notice there'll be less stuff coming out now, so this fresh bottle should hold you over until it's time to remove the drain. I expect that will be about one more week."

Mick and I were already very quickly learning that it is best not to have any expectations or plans of how things are supposed to be, because once you start planning, something is bound to happen. It's Murphy's law.

"Your shirt is wet," Mick commented later that night after my shower.

Having a shower with tubing and breast bandages is an interesting process, as you can't get any of it wet. While the hospital did provide me with giant plastic post-it notes to cover the wound sites, Mick and I found a much better alternative. Enter Glad Wrap. Yep, you heard right. I would strip off, stand with my arms outstretched as much as I was able, and then twirl around like a ballerina as Mick made me a boob tube of glad wrap. It worked a treat, provided I didn't stand full under the shower, the boobie bandages managed to stay fairly dry.

"I think I just got the bandages a little bit wet," I said, and finished eating my dinner with only my left hand, as my whole right side was still impossibly painful from the surgery less than a week ago. It could be from my long hair also, as no matter how hard I tried not to get it wet, it was impossible to tie up with one hand and even more impossible to dry if it got wet in the shower.

Mick looked at me in that way he has when he's not entirely convinced with the answer I gave. So under his watchful gaze, I stripped off my now sodden shirt to find to my surprise that the bandages were not actually shower wet, they were red all around where the drainage tube went in under my arm, and to top it off, there was absolutely nothing in the brand new bottle. Not a single drop and not a single floaty bit in either the bottle or the long tube. Instead of draining through the hose and into the bottle, it looked like I had sprung a leak all down my side, soaking up my bandages and my shirt.

"Hmmmm, that's not going to survive until the nurse comes in the morning," Mick looked very concerned. I could just imagine his brain thinking of blockages, infections, or perhaps even exploding boobs due to no drainage.

"Rug yourself up, we'd better go to the hospital and get this sorted before it becomes a bigger problem." So instead of settling in for a quiet night of TV, we headed off for the first of what would be many, impromptu visits throughout this journey, to the emergency department of Charlies.

"It looks like you have a defective bottle," explained the ER nurse shortly after we'd arrived at the hospital. "But that's an easy fix. We'll change you over to a fresh one, give you some clean dressings, and you'll be good to go."

Thankfully the rest of the drainage bottle experience, was uneventful. Even later on when I had four of these fashion accessories to carry around, it all seemed to go pretty well to plan. And let me tell you, carrying four 600ml bottles, slung over your shoulders, after you've just had major breast surgery, is not something you immediately associate with Breast Cancer. But one thing I was learning, is that this whole experience was not something either of us were prepared for.

Chapter 8
To Keep or Not to Keep

Everyone has a different name for them, knockers, boobs, breasts, titties, jugs, melons. I could use up a whole page with endearing terms for our prized assets. Our boobs have been used throughout history to define us as women, being squashed beyond recognition or proudly plumped depending on the fashions.

But regardless of who you are, or what you think about your boobs, being given the decision whether you'd like to keep them and risk death, or have them removed to live another day, is oddly not an easy decision to make. Especially when you've already been on an emotional roller coaster ride for the past month and are still in recovery from the most painful experience in your life. You would think that making a life or death decision would be a simple one, but when it comes to us women and our boobs - regardless of who we are - all common sense suddenly flies out the window.

And so, I found myself in the breast clinic with Mick beside me, having to make exactly this decision. Right now. There was no time to think about it.

"So just to go through this again, you understand the situation," my surgeon explained. "We took 14 nodes from your underarm. This is causing you pain and preventing you from lifting your arms above your head. They were all cancerous. In fact, some were so crusty they didn't really resemble being nodes anymore." Dr Yeo laughs at his own little joke. I wasn't laughing though, and neither was Mick.

"We took the cancerous growth from your breast and sent it off for testing. Unfortunately, the results showed we didn't get clear margins, meaning we didn't get all the cancer." His jovial manner switched back to serious again, probably because he saw we hadn't joined in on the light-hearted jokes. "That leaves us with a decision to make ... well ... you need to make a decision. Do we go back in and take a little extra, or do we remove the entire breast and nipple?"

"Take my boobs?" I protectively grabbed my boobs at the mere thought of losing them. One hand on each. While the thought of having them actually removed hadn't even occurred to me, the thought of having no nipples and no breasts at all just sounded absurd. I'd heard of having a mastectomy before. I didn't have my head buried in the sand. After all, I am a total information junky who works on the internet all day. But somewhere along the line I must have missed the bit about the nipples being removed as well. Why had nobody mentioned this to me? Why was this little bit of crucial information missing from my brain? And why did it suddenly seem so important to me?

"I want to keep my boobs, I like them." It's the only response I could come up with on such short notice. Needing to know I'd made the right decision, I looked to Mick for reassurance. He only shrugged the silent acknowledgement that it was my decision alone. He's never really been a boob man, just an ass man. I'm sure he would have an opinion if they said they were removing my ass cheeks.

I'm not the sort of girl who ever wears push up bras or shoves my boobs in people's faces to get what I want, although I will admit to taking subtle advantage of my ample supply to get a foot in the right door. My brain could not process the simple thought of my figure changing so dramatically that I would go from a DD cup to the appearance that my head had been put on backwards. If you can't comprehend what this looks like, grab a barbie doll and turn her head around to see what she looks like. I think if I was told that I would end up with "next to nothing" I could cope but having nothing at all is just too much to deal with.

I sit here now and wonder how to explain this, so a bloke understands the attachment every girl has to her boobs. Regardless of the type of girl, regardless of the size or shape, our boobs have been through a pretty important journey with us. You can't just remove them and expect us to carry on. Without them you have to re-learn to dress, sleep and be sexy. Like every other woman out there, my boobs and I have a long history together, with so many stories to tell.

As a young girl, you spend the first years approaching puberty wishing for big ones, wearing Mum's bra and stuffing it with oranges and tissues, then parading in front of the mirror imagining what it would be like. Then it's time for that first bra of your own and suddenly you wish they weren't so noticeable, because your body is changing, and you feel awkward instead of glamorous.

Approaching puberty, albeit later than many of the girls around me, my Mum was determined that I would not end up with saggy boobs. I pretty much had two options available to me, if family history was anything to go by. I would either be pretty small, or extremely large. So, at the delicate and extremely self-conscious age of 13, Mum marched me off to a lingerie store in the city. This store wasn't one of the pretty ones in the arcades with all the lace and colours, oh no, it was upstairs, away from the glam and sparkle. Apparently, they were the best for doing fittings.

'Fitting? You mean this old lady is going to see my boobs? AND TOUCH ME!!!!' Looking back, the old lady must have been well over 40. What would someone that old know about the type of bra a 13-year-old girl would need to wear so she didn't get teased in the sports change rooms?

And besides, even my own Mum didn't get to see me naked anymore. I didn't even look at myself in the mirror until I had clothes on. That would be so ... ewwwwww.

As a quiet and well-behaved girl, I only protested to my Mum with wide open and pleading eyes as I followed the old lady with her arm full of little bras. I passed another wistful glance back at my Mum in the hope that she would rescue me from this absolute indignity before

I disappeared forever into the change rooms. But oh no! She wasn't even looking at me. She was looking at bras for herself. And not the fuddy duddy ones like she picked out for me, she was looking at pretty ones with lace.

So now that I had a bra, I had to actually wear it to school. It was so obvious that I had a bra, as everyone could see the lines through my white school t-shirt, and I really didn't even have boobs yet. My first bra was sized 8AAA also known as a "training bra." I had nothing to train. Not like the other girls at school. The amount of padding made me look like I had suddenly grown these huge boobs over the weekend. Friday, I went home from school with no boobs, Monday I turned up for school with massive boobs out there for everyone to see.

Kerpling! That sudden sound accompanied by a sharp pain as my bra strap was pinched back and then let go with a snap by one of the boys in my class. I spun around only to see him laughing with his mates. I could feel my face turn a hot shade of red which only amused them even more, which in turn changed the red to burgundy. I stormed off embarrassed at the personal attack and tried to find a quiet corner where I could re-adjust my bra back into a semi comfortable position. Wearing a bra was just so uncomfortable, so it didn't help that it needed to be adjusted after being plucked like a guitar string every time I went anywhere near a group of boys. But like every other teenage girl, I survived high school without any permanent scarring on my back from the constant snaps, and to my Mum's relief, I did not end up with giant saggy boobs. I'm sure she still charts that up to forcing me to wear a bra so early.

These days, when you visit any shopping centre you will see lingerie shops on every corner, instead of being hidden upstairs and out of sight. And there are all types of bras available for every size and shape breast, including pretty ones for beginners. But of course, you know that, but did you know that there is also a place called the Boob Gallery? I'm not kidding, it's a real place where you can see the results of different mastectomy and reconstruction surgeries on different body shapes and sizes. It's not like you can actually choose which boobs you want, but Mick still managed to have a bit of fun with the idea of the gallery.

"Can I come and choose your new boobs?" Mick asked me when I explained the gallery.

"But I thought you were and arse man, not a boob man."

"Hey, who am I to miss out on the opportunity. They're my new toy, so it should be my choice," he justified himself to me.

"Yeh, and if I leave it to you, they'll be huge and impractical."

I had finally come to terms with the fact that I would have to have one of my boobs removed. During a second surgery the cancerous lump had been removed, but in the process more cancer was found. The decision was taken out of my hands and I was simply told that a mastectomy was now going to happen. I would have plenty of time to come to terms with the idea and say my farewells, as the surgery was now being planned for after all my cancer treatment.

Together over many nights and many glasses of wine, Mick and I finally came to the only decision that felt right for both of us. I would have both boobs removed after finishing chemo and radiation, and then go with a silicone reconstruction. This decision wasn't just about removing the fear of the cancer returning in the other boob. Part of the choice was to have a symmetrical pair, and also to choose the quickest option for recovery with the least amount of surgery. This option also meant I would be back out on that drag racing track sooner rather than later.

Chapter 9

Shave it, Pluck it, Wax it

How much do you love having hair? I do, well, I thought I did. Most of my life, mine has been long, extremely thick, blonde and straight. Sure, I left it everywhere and on everything, and if I didn't tie it up at night, I'd not only smother myself in my sleep but also Mick. I've spent a fortune over the years keeping it blonde as it has slowly gone darker and darker. I've spent exorbitant amounts on products to keep it straight and smooth and in place. To this day I still have a bathroom drawer full of curling wands, hair dryers, straightening irons, pins, clips, bows and tiebacks that I can't seem to part with.

I have spent hour after hour in front of the mirror designing styles and preparing for a night out.

After my first surgery, I found out something pretty startling about my hair that I'd never had the opportunity to find out before. My wonderful, very handy around the house husband cannot do a simple hair plait or even tie a ponytail with an elastic band. Who knew it was that complicated?

So following a couple of major surgeries, one of which I was left unable to lift my arms up over my head for over a month, I can now admit to having some seriously bad hair days. At that point I didn't even have any hats or scarves to wear.

With chemo just around the corner, and a pretty radical treatment agreed upon with the oncologist, my best friend Sue decided that she wouldn't let me go it alone. This is what best friends are all about. Sue lives over 3000km away from me in the North West, but still felt it was her duty as a true and honest friend, to be there in person for the ultimate haircut and then scarf and hat shop.

"You nervous?" asked Sue.

I felt the butterflies in my stomach making themselves known as we drove to the hairdresser.

"I dunno," I lied "maybe a little excited. It's just great having you in Perth to spend the day with. I'm not even really thinking about everything else."

We had a full day planned all in preparation for Chemo. There was the haircut, then a little pampering with a nice lunch, followed by a little shopping, then we planned to top it off with a trip to the "hair and hat" shop for some head warmers and no hair hiders. If you can't trust your best friend to be honest about how you'll look bald and, in a beanie, who can you trust?

Arriving at the hairdresser, Jamie-Lee looked just as

nervous about doing the "big cut" as I felt. I guess it would be a hard job for a hairdresser, making such a drastic change to someone's look, especially if they had been giving that person the exact same hairstyle for near on 5 years as Jamie-Lee had been with me.

"How short will we go?" Jamie-Lee asked me as she held out the freshly washed ponytail and poised the scissors around shoulder height.

"Oh no! Much shorter than that." I thought Sue was going to grab the scissors and do the cutting herself. She flicked a magazine to a page with P!nk on it and tapped the page. "This short."

"Are you sure?" Jamie-Lee worriedly asked me.

"y-Yes," I stammered trying to sound more confident than I felt. "It's all going to fall out anyway."

"That's the way, girlfriend." Sue smiled at my reflection in the mirror. I'm not sure if she couldn't see how terrified I was, or she just chose to ignore my fear the way only a best friend can. As Jamie-Lee was about to cut the ponytail off, Sue got the camera out.

"Give me a totally horrified look for the camera, Andy," Sue laughed. Like I had to try.

SNIP!

The ponytail was gone. Jamie-Lee laid it on top of the magazines, and immediately Sue rushed over with the camera to take a picture of that also. In fact, while Jamie-Lee was busy snipping away, Sue was busy clicking away with the camera, only taking time out to say, "more off, much shorter".

And then it was Sue's turn.

"Just a little trim for me," she stated as the apron was placed around her shoulders.

"Oh, you bitch," I scoffed at her. "You made me think you were going to get it cut short to match."

"Paul would divorce me if I came home with short hair," she joked, but smiled at me. "But yours looks awesome."

"Fine!" I did the pretend sulk. "You just wait, I'll get my pay back."

As it turned out, the new hairstyle, as great as it did look, didn't last long before the tell-tale signs of chemo began to ravage my system. It's the one thing everyone knows about. Chemo makes your hair fall out. The truth is, not all chemo does, but my regime kept its promise to let me see if I had any scars on my head that needed an explanation from Mum and Dad.

Shopping for hats and scarves while you still have hair is an interesting experience, but I certainly wasn't going to wait for my hair to fall out to do it. I really wanted to be prepared. And who better to help with the ultimate fashion trip than a best friend who is not afraid to tell you the honest truth.

"No way, you'll look like a sick granny in that," Sue said loud enough for the whole hair and hat shop to hear. I thought the lady behind the counter was going to come and tell her off for being so critical towards me. "Here, try this one" and she handed me a really nice tartan baggy cap with a peak. "And I know you said no wigs, but this is just a fringe."

I tried on the hair piece headband with the cap over the top.

"Hey that looks pretty cool. I don't think anyone will notice I don't have hair with this on." Half a dozen caps, scarves and beanies later I was set to rock the world of baldness. Going bald was not going to be a problem because I had people around me to make sure I wasn't going to look like a victim. I had friends who would be on the lookout to make sure I looked my best, even at my worst.

About a week after my first round of chemo, I noticed that the hair on my head wasn't really hair anymore, it was like it had died and was just hanging around. Gradually each hair follicle began to hurt so much that I took to wearing a beanie that was kindly supplied in the recent Street Machine magazine, to stop my hair from even just moving around. But it still hurt, and it was starting to come out in large handfuls.

"It's time for the shave, hun," I let Mick know. We had discussed over the past week that when I was ready, Mick would get out the trimmers and give me the number 1 all over. While I was eager to get it over and done with, it's not every day you get your head shaved, so I couldn't keep the experience to myself. I setup the video camera, carefully balanced on a box of tissues and set ready to record. Then I setup the laptop and connected skype to my best friend Sue.

"Hey chickie, are you ready for the big shave?" I asked.

"You bet," I heard the chorus of Sue and the rest of the family sitting around a laptop. "You go girl. We're all here with you."

"Well madame, if you would like to sit on zee chair, I shall do my very best to give you ze latest fashion 'air style," Mick waived the clippers about in the stereotypical comedic gay French hairdresser style, his accent akin to Rene from 'Allo 'Allo.

Buzz, buzz, buzz. Mick appeared to be having a ball.

"A little bit of 'ere, and a little bit of dere."

Without my glasses on I was totally at his mercy. I couldn't see what everyone else could see and he was totally playing the part for his audience.

"Ooooo madame, did you know about zis scar on your 'ead?"

"Really? I have a scar on my head?" I wasn't sure if he was joking or not.

"Ooooo, never mind, I am sure there will be more when I 'av finished."

Buzz, buzz, buzz.

So much hair was falling to the floor. I couldn't believe I still had this much left considering how much had already fallen out.

"Oh wow," voices came out of the computer from my onlookers, "You look beautiful". I wasn't accepting that as a truth. Skinny, pasty faced and now bald. I was certainly not feeling at all beautiful, but for some reason I was still smiling. I could feel the huge cheesy grin on my face, and I could not stop with the hysterical giggling.

"Zar you go madame, vould you like to 'av a look?"

"Us first" I heard those voices again. "Turn around and show us."

So I did the slow turn for the camera feeling my head at the same time. I had no idea how much was gone and could only feel it was quite prickly. Then Mick held up the mirror for me to see the result. Immediately my hands shot up to cover my mouth at the shock of seeing myself with next to no hair. It wasn't all gone, but there were some major bald patches mixed in with only what I could call stubble.

I looked up at Mick, who was now standing there with a silly accomplished grin on his face. Well I guess I couldn't blame him. It's not every day a bloke gets to shave his woman's head. So, there we were, both of us with super shaved heads. Actually, I think I now had less hair than him, since a number 3 is Micks standard cut.

Overwhelmed by the emotion of the moment, I reached up, one hand on each side of his face. I pulled Mick down to me and gave him the biggest kiss.

"Thank you, babe."

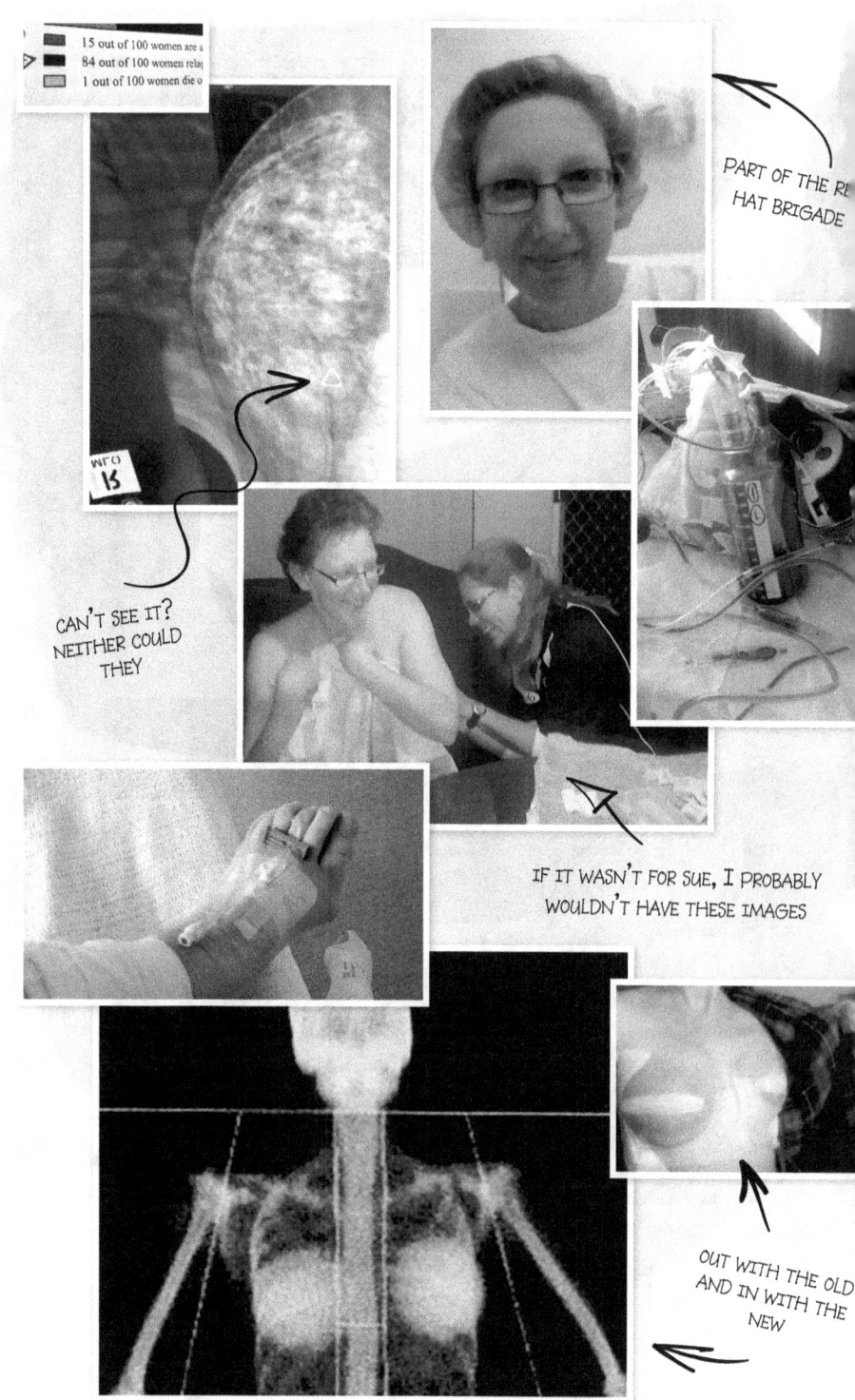

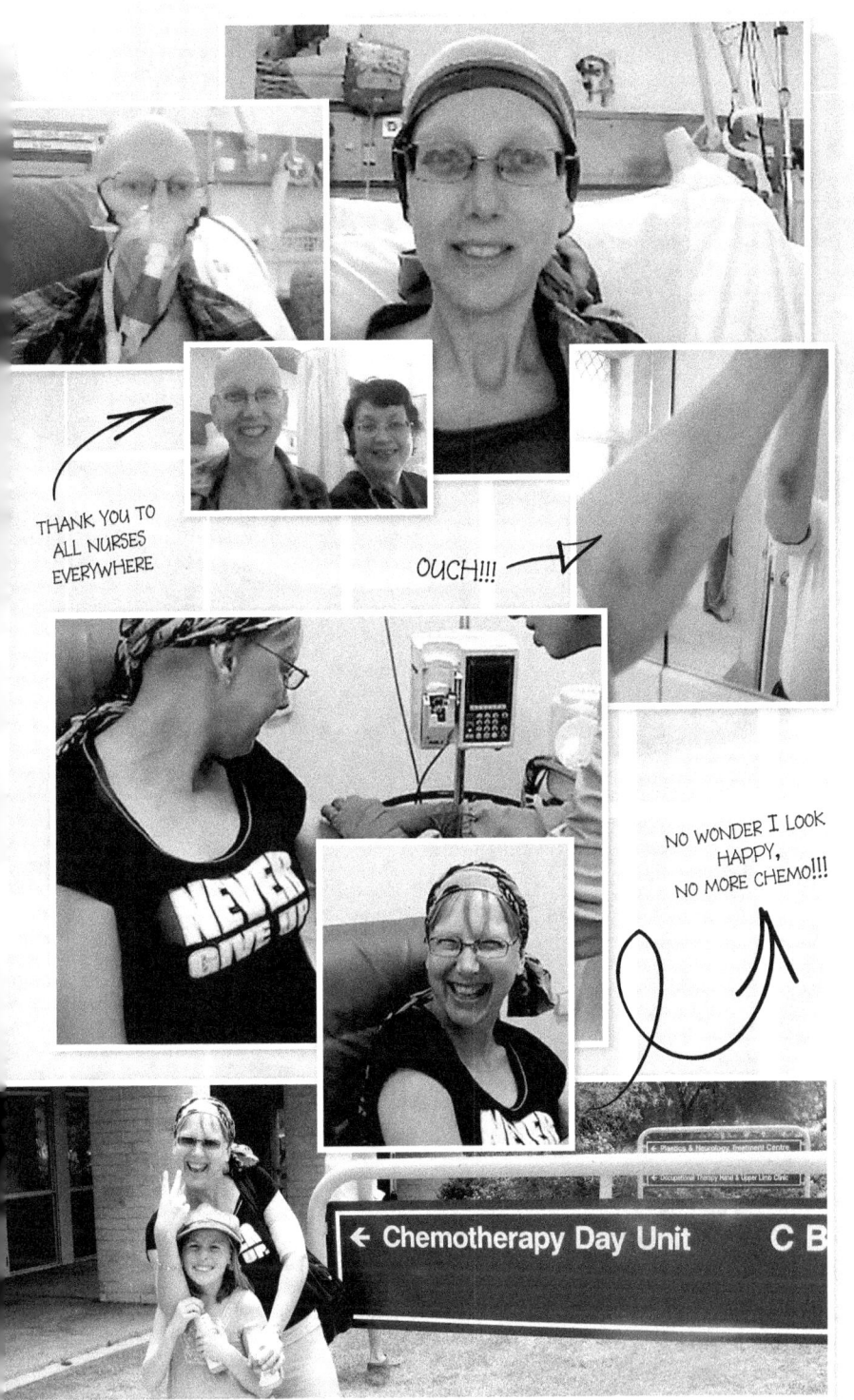

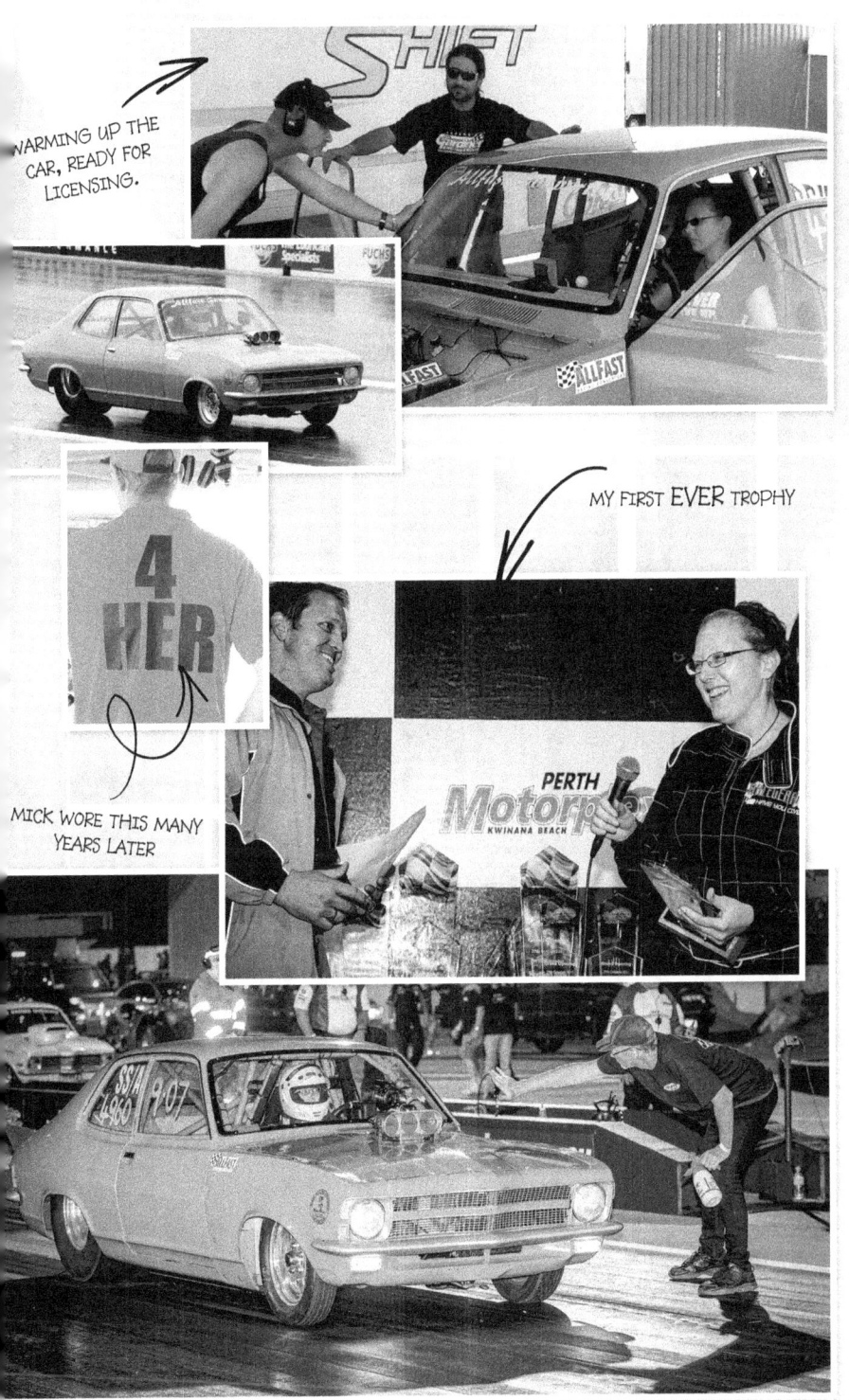

I DON'T NEED A TROPHY TO FEEL LIKE I'M A WINNER

Chapter 10
The Red Devil

As Mick and I walked in the front door of the chemotherapy lounge for the very first time, I was like a new kid at school. I stopped and took in my new surroundings. The sounds, sights and smells.

The chemo area rooms were really not what I expected, although I'm not sure what I was actually anticipating. It seemed a lot more upbeat than any other part of the hospital that I have seen. Perhaps that was why they had been set up away from the rest, down in the basement.

At first, I noticed there was music playing. Not elevator music. Real music at the level you play in your own house. My eyes looked for the source and I saw 2 young nurses dancing in the corridor with a chemo patient who was still attached to her IV tube. The others around them were laughing along as if dancing in the hospital corridor was a totally natural thing to do.

A lady bounded through the door we'd just entered, wearing a huge smile, the brightest pink wig I've ever seen, and carrying a massive tray of cupcakes with bright pink icing. Her hubby followed just behind her with arms full of gift bags and balloons covered in bright pink ribbon.

"Whoohoo, last chemo today. I made it through," she cheered to the nurses, and looked directly at me, the stunned rabbit stuck in the headlights.

"You'll make it too, hun. Just take it one chemo at a time, and you'll be celebrating like me before you know it."

Off she skipped after one of the nurses, handing out cakes and gifts on her way to the big comfy chemo infusion chairs.

And so began my journey ... THE morning of THE Day had finally arrived.

Not surprisingly, neither of us had got much sleep the previous night, and I for one, was awake much too early. While Mick headed off to work for a couple of hours, I had spent the morning trying to be as normal and calm as possible. I changed the sheets and did a little housework. I was certain I would not feel like doing this later, so did it all while I still felt well.

My Oncologist, Dr 'Geezer', had decided that due to the nasty bully nature of my particular strain of cancer, "we" needed to go in hard with a new recipe of chemo that had just come off trial in the US, but hadn't been used in Australia yet.

Now call me naïve, but I thought chemotherapy was just one drug. I didn't realise it was actually a treatment consisting of a whole cocktail of different drugs, depending on the recipe your oncologist uses. So, my recipe meant that we would have to visit this crazy lounge every two weeks for about 4 months, the two intervening weeks would apparently allow my body enough time to recover before coming back.

The patient chairs in the chemo lounge are like great big old-fashioned barbers chairs, the type you just want to kick out that footrest and relax. I sat back in mine, and immediately felt like I was being swallowed up in a great big hug, while Mick stared with jealousy at my comfort and parked himself beside me in a plastic chair.

"First time?" a nurse grabbed my arm and started looking for a vein, giving gentle taps. She was cheerful, friendly and made me feel instantly calmer.
"You'll be fine, and it'll be all over before you know it." In no time she had my veins sticking out loud and proud.

"It looks like you have some good veins there, Andrea, or do you prefer Andy?"
Wow, no-one at the hospital had ever asked me that before.

"I prefer Andy."

I melted into her calmness, not even realising that she had put the needle and line into my arm. These are some very special nurses, I realised, who are not just good at their jobs but are also capable of making you feel like you belong and at ease.

I watched her purple gloved hands as she gently flushed my cannula to check it was working, then connected up my first bag of drugs with the big biohazard warning sticker on it.

"Now you just sit back and enjoy the ride. If you feel at all weird, let me know. And any questions either of you have no matter how silly you might think they are, just ask."

She stripped off the purple gloves and apron, handed Mick the TV remote.

"I'm guessing you will be needing this more than Andy."

It wasn't long before I did have a silly question after coming back from the toilet, but I wasn't sure how to broach the subject. I didn't even want to mention it to Mick, in case he got all worried. It was really personal, and the nurse seemed too nice for me to share something so weird and so obviously wrong with my body. So, I waited for her to come over and check my IV.

"My pee is red," I quietly whispered, terrified that something was horribly wrong, and I'd be whisked off to surgery. Code Blue, Code Red, Code Purple, drop everything, Andy has red pee.

The nurse smiled with a light reassuring laugh, "That's just the bright red chemo drug going through your system. Just the same as if you were to drink heaps and heaps of red cordial. That's also why we have a different toilet for chemo patients. We wouldn't want to expose the nurses or visitors to these drugs, would we?"

She tucked me back into my armchair with a blanket straight from the warmer. It was like she already knew, without me having to say anything, that the chemo being pumped into me felt like iced water running through my veins. A visible shiver went through me. Even though I was warm on the outside, I felt cold as ice on the inside. I don't know if it was the drugs, the lack of sleep the previous night, the seriously hectic day I had had with appointments and tests. I couldn't believe this experience would use up an entire day.

Maybe it was just the nice warm blanket. As I laid there, Mick at my side watching the tv, I drifted off into a light doze. Still aware of the movement around me, I felt at peace and didn't even open my eyes when the nurse came to remove my cannula and send me home.

Once Mick and I got home several hours later, we both simply crashed into bed. I couldn't keep my eyes open. I actually felt a little heady, like I'd just had a couple too many wines, so I chose to skip dinner.

Actually, it's not that I really chose to skip it, I just didn't feel well enough to eat. You know that feeling when you're not quite car sick, but you can feel it coming on? You know that one more bump or whiff of KFC through the window and you're a goner. So off to bed I went with an empty tummy for a totally exhausted dreamless sleep.

Halfway through the night, probably around midnight, but I didn't stop to check the clock, I woke to find my gut churning. I took a few deep breaths, trying to will my body and my stomach to calm down, but it didn't work.

'Slow breathing, deep breathing, you'll be OK,' I kept telling myself. 'You'll be fine, just relax.'

NOPE ... RUNNNNNNNNN for the bathroom.

Breakfast, Lunch, Dinner, and even that little piece of pink cake I had from the lady celebrating her last chemo, all came back to say hello.

And my nose was also running.

Grabbing some toilet paper, I stuffed it up my nose, but it was pouring out faster than I could soak it up. And since I was still heaving, I was trying to work out how I could breathe out of my ears.

I finally looked down at the collection of soaking toilet paper in my hand and saw that my nose wasn't just running … it was bleeding. I didn't know what to do.

So, I started to cry. No sound, just tears streaming down my face. I was sitting on the cold floor in my undies and tank top, hugging the toilet, heaving the lining of my stomach into the bowl, shoving toilet paper up my nose and crying in absolute and total self-pity.

Mick turned the light on to see me sitting on the cold floor, shivering, nose bleeding, dry heaving, sweating, and crying. I looked up at him through my tears. "I don't feel very good."

He draped my dressing gown over my shoulders, leaned over and flushed my last meals away.

"I'll make you a cup of tea. Come out when you think you can."

I stuffed some fresh toilet paper up my nose, struggled into my dressing gown and with some effort lifted myself up onto shaky legs. Terrified that any sudden movement would set me off again, I ever so gently shuffled to what was soon to be my favourite spot on the couch. Mick handed me a mug of tea and some anti-nausea meds.

"Take these, then try to have some tea." He put a blanket over me and turned on the TV. He was so gentle, and so caring, and all I could think about was how sick I felt, how my head hurt, how tired I felt, how weak my body felt.

Why did it take so much effort to hold my tea? I guessed this was the "chemo fatigue" they all talked about. It was a feeling far beyond tired. It was a feeling far beyond exhaustion even. I had never felt so weary that I was unable to even look or listen, but that was how I felt.

I had become an aching, sweaty, shivering, vomiting, bleeding, vegetable who would soon also be bald and have no boobs. Somehow, I still had enough strength left in me for tears, no sobs, just quiet totally self-pitying tears.

Chapter 11
You'll Feel a Little Scratch

I donate blood and plasma, but I don't like needles. I'd like to say I donate out of the goodness of my heart, but I actually feel obliged to donate because I have a rare blood type, and the chances are pretty good that either I'll need that blood back myself or one of my family will. It's not too bad if I don't see the needle going in, but somehow if I get to see that skin being pierced, the pain of the needle triples. So, when I found out that I was going to have to give myself an injection every couple of weeks, I went into total denial, and told myself it wouldn't be a problem at all.

"You'll be ok," I told myself bravely when I sat in the dining room with a needle in one hand and a handful of belly in the other. Mick was also very encouraging at my first attempt at self-injection.

"If you can't do it, I'm quite happy to throw a dart at your belly," he offered with not quite an evil grin, but he

certainly did appear to be much too enthusiastic.
"I really should be able to do this myself, but my brain won't let my hand do it," I complained. It was like when your mouse on the computer freezes, it just wasn't moving.

"Like I said," Mick offered again, but this time with a little more seriousness, "If you want me to give it a go…"

So I did. I absolutely hate giving in, but I had to admit I'd lost this challenge. I handed over the needle, let go of my belly, screwed up my face in anticipation and looked away.

"OOOOWWWWWWW!!!!!! I'm not a dartboard!!!" I screamed, rubbing the spot just below my belly button where the needle had gone in. "Did you even look? or did you just throw it?"

"Hey, I didn't say I would be good at it, I just said I would do it." Mick tossed the needle into the bright yellow sharps bin on top of the fridge. But exactly two weeks later Mick came virtually skipping into the lounge room with a needle in one hand and a cotton swab in the other.

"Time to bare the belly, I need target practice."

"Are you really enjoying this?" I asked him incredulously.

"Of course not," Mick smiled his cheeky grin back at me as he grabbed a fresh piece of belly to pierce. "I take absolutely no pleasure at all in watching you squirm."

"OOOOWWWWWWW!!!!!! and you're not improving with your aim much either," I complained.

"Well, looking at the bruise from last week, I reckon I might be able to create a dot to dot picture on your belly,"

Mick laughed.

And he wasn't far from wrong either. Every needle I received, whether it was for injections or donations, would leave a huge bruise, so I was really starting quite the collection.

"I've received word back that you have very skinny and wiggly veins," Dr Geeza (my oncologist) informed me following my first chemo week. Skinny and wiggly? I guess that explains why the vampires pull that face when I bare my arm for inspection and donation. "So, I've booked you in to get a PICC line installed before your next chemo."

'Cool,' I thought. 'No more needles.' But how wrong I was.

A PICC line is kind of like a cannula, but you get to keep it in for months. The only problem with having something like that sitting around on the outside of your body is that you can't get it dirty, you can't get it wet, and you can't feed it after midnight .... I hadn't actually tried feeding it after midnight, but I did find out you can't feed it when it's sick. No matter how hard you try to keep it dry and clean, when your immune system is bombing out down in the low single digits, an infection is quite likely to happen.

"You've picked up a bug in your PICC line," I was told barely weeks after having it installed. "It's not a reflection on your cleanliness or anything, it just happens sometimes. But we will need to take it out, and you'll have to stay in hospital for a little while."

Great, I'd barely had a chance to use it, and they were already calling in the defect warranty on my direct line to the fortnightly poison. This didn't mean I was going to miss out on the fortnightly injections though, no such luck, and in addition to the chemo, I was now getting twice daily blood tests and multiple antibiotic and saline feeds, all into the one and only arm I had available for any such work. Due to having all those lymph nodes removed from the right armpit, that arm was now not allowed to be used for blood pressure checks or needles.

Squeak, squeak, squeak, I can hear the tell-tale sound of the vampires and their trolley coming down the hospital corridor. Without even thinking, I pull the sleeves of my flanny down to cover my arms and slide down as far as I can under the covers of my hospital bed. 'Please don't stop here, please don't stop here,' I start chanting quietly under my breath, in the desperate hope that I'm not their next victim. SQUEAK SQUEAK SQUEAK, the sound increases torturing my senses, until I finally see the flash of chrome as the trolley turns into my hospital room.

"Hi Andy," the vampire shows her big toothy smile, "how is that arm of yours holding up?" I had already had 2 weeks of needles several times a day, along with an often-relocating cannula.

I sighed and resigned myself to the fact that hiding under the covers isn't going to help, and pull myself up into a sitting position on the bed, sliding my left sleeve up at the same time to reveal a no longer pale white arm, but instead one with a patchwork of bluish grey and yellow hues. Not only was my arm displaying the colourful results, but it was also feeling the pain of every single 'you'll just feel a little pinch'. In addition to the bruising, one of the vampire's favourite veins had collapsed, now mimicking a tightly wound guitar string running all the way up my left arm.

"Oooooo, that looks painful," the nurse showed heartfelt concern at sighting the condition of my arm, accompanied by the pained look on my face as I carefully straightened out the tightened vein, worried that if I stretched it too suddenly, "PLINK" it would snap. "I'll be really gentle, and hopefully we can find an available spot, so we don't have to venture down to your feet."

MY FEET? I don't even like getting a foot massage or pedicure, and they were talking about drawing blood from my feet? My feet are mega, super sensitive, and you want to go in there with a sharp needle? I could feel myself quietly and carefully wrapping the sheets around my feet while the nurse was distracted surveying my arm. There was no way I was giving up my feet without a fight.

Little did I realise that much later in my treatment I would be walking around with a cannula in the top of one of my feet. Apparently if you have a surgeon working on both sides of your chest, the Anaesthetist prefers to stay out of his way, heading instead for the feet.

Even though it turns out having a cannula in the top of your foot is more of an inconvenience than a pain, I still won't allow anyone near my feet.

Chapter 12
The Euphoria of Feeling Normal

"I'm bored.... oh boy I am so bored."

There must be something else I could do around the house. I'd watched every movie, I'd read heaps of books, I did several crossword puzzles, and I even cooked up such a storm that the freezer was totally full of homemade "tv dinners". The house was clean. I'd even washed the windows.

It's easy to assume cancer and chemo patients are sick all the time, although you'd probably be surprised to learn the actual truth can be quite the opposite.

Sure, I would have some seriously down days where talking myself into getting out of bed in the morning, even if it was just to relocate to the couch would be a chore. But then there would be these comparatively good days which would make me want to conquer the entire world all in one day, just in case I didn't get the opportunity to do it again.

Unfortunately, that feeling would be quickly overwhelmed by sheer exhaustion and at the end of the day I would fall asleep on the couch before dinner time, albeit with a smile.

So, what could I do?

Well, really there was only one thing left to do. I would just have to go out. Yes, out there in the big wide world of the local shopping centre. Without hair. WITHOUT HAIR? Oh no, I might have been happy about going commando at home, but there was no way I would do it OUT THERE ... So, the search was on to find something to wear on my head. Where was that pretty silk scarf?

I bet you didn't know that by not having any hair at all, you can actually double your "getting ready" time in the bathroom. Scarf in hand I twirled it and swirled it, knotted it, tied it in a bow. But without hair to hold the scarf in place, there was no way it was going to stay in place.

Say hello to YouTube. You so have to love the internet. How did cancer patients learn stuff like how to wear a scarf on a bald head before the invention of the internet? I watched the video clip over and over, sat in front of the mirror and twisted, twirled, knotted and eventually gave up in favour of a hat with my little fake fringe. I did a quick last-minute check in the mirror by the front door before I left the house. Pushed my shoulders back, my chest out, and held my head high. I looked great. I was feeling great. I'd made the effort to get dressed up, and even added a little make-up to hide my oddly grey coloured face and dark circles. I was positive no-one would be able to see I was sick.

I jumped in the driver's seat for the first time in what seemed like an age.

'Easy does it' I told myself, 'your brain is not quite as reactive as it should be.' Even though my little Tiida isn't at all powerful, I still drove like an old lady who'd borrowed her grandson's sup'ed up V8, and probably annoyed every person on the road around me.

I arrived safely, at what used to be claimed as the largest shopping centre in the Southern Hemisphere, just the same. I picked the easiest parking spot, with plenty of distance between me and all the other vehicles, but "crunch"... whoops, that would be the front bumper on the curb. 'Not a problem, just back it up a little' ... sssscraaaaapeeee ...

Now it was time to go shopping. I'm sure I did a little excited skip through the carpark. I have to admit, I was pretty excited, and I'm sure everyone could see the manic grin on my face. It felt like it had been so long since I had felt well enough to venture out into the real world. Even though I didn't have anything I wanted to buy, and since I hadn't been working, I didn't have much to spend either. Still I strutted from shop to shop, not missing a single display table decked out with specials that would only be out there for just that one day. All the colours were so much richer and brighter than usual, just like after a fresh rain. And every child seemed to be smiling, so I would give a big hearty smile and a wink back.

Kids are awesome, they are little mirrors to our own feelings. The bakery was pumping out some tantalizing smells, making me wonder if I should risk having a sticky bun with pink icing special for breast cancer fundraising? But I decided that the lack of effective tastebuds wouldn't allow me to enjoy it. At least I could enjoy the smell. At least my nose hadn't gone on holiday.

Humming along to the music in Target while browsing and getting in everyone's way, was the perfect way to enjoy the normality of everything. But there was something different. I could see it out of the corner of my eye. It wasn't direct, only allowing me to see an occasional glimpse. But even if I couldn't look at it direct, I knew it was there.

People were looking at me with sadness in their eyes. Why would they do that? Couldn't they see I was feeling great? They should have been happy for me. I forced an even bigger smile and looked right at the next person I walked past. But they averted their gaze very quickly. Dam them, couldn't they see I was happy?

Well, I had started out happy, but my smile was quickly fading, and I didn't feel like being out in public anymore.

"Such a beautiful hat," an elderly lady commented as she walked past me. But I could see her eyes were saying, "Such a brave girl." I didn't feel brave. You can't be brave doing something you have no choice about.

The odour of fatty food was starting to turn my stomach, and that tuneless muzak was making my ears ring. I started to move towards the shop exit through a throng of so many people, all pushing, shoving and talking loudly. Some even pulled their screaming children away from the freaky lady with no hair.

"Don't stare at her, she has cancer," I thought I could hear them whisper just out of earshot "poor girl, so brave." I needed to get out of there, as it was not fun anymore. I wanted to go home to my couch.

"Oh why did I have to park so far away?" I grumbled to myself, as I dragged my tiring body through the carpark. It felt like it was such a long way to walk in the hot bright sun. Shopping centres should have a little shuttle bus like they do at the hospital car park.

Scratch, scratch. My head was starting to itch under my fake fringe and hat, making me want to rip the hat off as soon as I got in the car to let my head breathe. I didn't care anymore if anyone saw me. I just wanted to close my eyes.

"Come on … not much further …" I encouraged myself to keep going until I finally made it home.

"Hey babe," Mick was gently waking me up to a cold dark house. "You haven't been lying here all day, have you?"

"No." I eased myself into a sitting position and tried to get my bearings back.

"I felt good this morning, so I went to the shops." Mick smiled proudly, "did you have fun?"

"It was great," a yawn snuck out. "I think I over did it though."

"Well, you go have a shower and freshen up while I make you some dinner. Then you can go back to bed."

I think that was the best offer I'd had all day.

***

You would think that experience would have made me think twice about heading out again into the big wide world of the shopping centre. But oh no, when you've been stuck inside day after day, the need for stimulation becomes so overpowering that you might even forget that you're sick. For a little while at least.

"I'm going to watch Gonzo do his 8 seconds in the GT at the drags this afternoon."

Hubby was also extremely eager to get out of the sick house and into a world of methanol, burnouts and revving engines.

"Do you think you might be up to coming along?"

I had been feeling pretty good for over a week, so it sounded like a great idea to me. And I'd been missing my drag racing friends too. Packing for an outing with a chemo patient is like packing for a baby. If you want to have the best chance of enjoying yourself for the longest time possible, you need to cater for every eventuality. So, we packed warm clothing, lots of water, some snacks, sunscreen, earplugs, a big sun hat, scarf, light shirt with long sleeves, anti-nausea tablets, Panadol, lip balm, dark sunglasses, Aeroguard, a rug, fold up chairs, camera, phone. Did we miss anything?

"What's the worst that can happen," Mick said cheerfully on the way down to the racetrack.
"If you get really tired or the noise is too much for you, we turn around and go home again."

You really couldn't argue with that kind of logic, now, could you? Heading through the Motorplex gates, all my senses went into total overload. The sound of v8 engines tuned to perfection, the smell of various different blends of race fuel, the sound and smell of tyres being warmed up on the burnout pad, the sizzle of barbecues throughout the pit area.

Oh! how much I had missed this place. My second home. I totally forgot about being bald and having a PICC line hanging out of my arm. Immediately, I started to see familiar faces that I had not seen in so long, and they were not looking at me with pity. They were excited to see me. Great big "awesome to see ya" smiles, massive rib crushing hugs willing me to be strong and powerful. I was feeling strong and vibrant from all the energy being willed through to me from my racing family.

So I split my day up fluttering about the pit area, chatting to racers and friends and kicking back on the grass to watch the drag racing. My smile could not have been bigger, and my heart could not have pounded any harder with the enjoyment of the day.

Mick would regularly catch up with me throughout the day to check how I was doing.

"You're drinking lots of water? Making sure you rest? Taking time out of the sun? Are you hungry? If you're tired you know where to find me, we'll go home."

What did I do to deserve such a doting hubby like this! "I'm fine. I'm taking it easy." I assured him. "And besides, I can just sleep all day tomorrow to make up for it. I'm having fun."

The truth was I was in ecstasy and I didn't feel sick at all.

Mick smiled that true happiness smile that you have when you see someone else so truly happy and headed off to hang out in the pits with his mates. Sitting back on the grass in a nice shady spot under the commentators' box, it felt like I had been there for hours and hours, running around, catching up with old friends. But when I looked at my watch, I was shocked to see that it had only been about two hours since we walked through the gates. I could feel my body crashing. Weariness washed over me like a big heavy blanket. When that wave of exhaustion starts to wash over you, what comes with it is the realization that you could sleep on the runway and not be woken by a jet plane.

'I'll just sit and quietly watch some racing, and if I doze off, so be it,' I thought. I so didn't want to spoil Micks day. An arm curled around my shoulders. "Ready to head home?" Mick had come to check on me, and although I wasn't sleeping, I wasn't "with" it either. He could see it in my face. I had switched into zombie mode.

"Sure" I smiled weakly back at him, it had been a day to remember, even if I had only lasted a couple of hours.

Chapter 13
Angels in Comfortable Shoes

To the ones who cleaned my wounds,
took me to the toilet, bathed me
To the night angels who comforted me when I was
afraid.
To the ones who danced and sang,
and laughed at my silly jokes.
To the night angels who were there when I was
scared.
To the ones who gave me needles,
and the ones who tried to find veins
To the ones who gave me oxygen and told me not to
be afraid.
I can see it in your eyes,
your tiredness and your pain
But your heart shows through, and your emotion
can be seen

The twinge of sadness for me
Your brave smile to my family
You are a human angel, and I am only me.
~Andy

Chemo was cancelled today.

You would think I would be happy with this announcement from my doctor. No poison today. But no, I am not happy because I will still have to have the same amount of chemo rounds, it'll now just take longer to be finished. And the quicker they were done and dusted, the quicker I would get back to a normal life and start racing again. I couldn't afford delays in my treatment. I was on my own little schedule to be well and back at the racetrack before the season was finished.

Sure, I'd been running a temperature for over a week. Mick had even arranged for my Mum to come over during the day and "Andy-sit" while he was at work. Anything over 38 degrees is an automatic hospital admission for cancer patients. Mine hadn't quite reached that point, although it was higher than normal, and I did look and feel lousy. According to the doctor this dose dense chemo regime they had me on had knocked me about a bit too much, so an additional week of recovery would be required. I may also have picked up a mild case of the flu.

"Just rug up and have lots of chicken soup," he suggested.

Just as well Mick had taken some time out from looking after me to spend a little time in the kitchen making chicken soup, from scratch. He's pretty clever like that.

So, I sat on the couch, vegetating to something totally watch worthy on tv, sweating away through my little fever, keeping the fluids up and eating chicken soup.

'phew I stink... or is that just my chemo sensitive nose overreacting again.'

I thought that even though I'd just had a shower I could already really use another one … But rugged up in my blanket I didn't feel in the mood to expose my bare skin to the cold air. While the blanket didn't help much in keeping me warm, it was still warmer with, than without. A shiver raked through my aching body and I pulled the blanket tighter to warm the outside and had another sip of chicken soup to try and warm the inside.

With not enough energy to keep my eyes open, I decided to just close them briefly and listen to the tv.

Ahhhh. Sleeeeeeeeep.

"Honey" I felt Mick fussing about me. "Honey I need to take your temperature."

"mmmm, wha... urgh" Why would he want to wake me up in the middle of the night.

"Babe" He was getting more serious "It's 11 o'clock in the morning and you've been asleep since yesterday afternoon."

He couldn't be serious. But why would he lie about something like that?

"mmmm, wha... urgh" I tried to roll over ready to sleep more, only there was a firm hand on my shoulder shaking me to wake up. OK, this was getting beyond a joke, why couldn't he just leave me alone.

"WHAT!" I opened my eyes and scowled at him with the angriest face I could muster.

"Your temp is almost 40 and you look like you've been swimming." Mick was not accepting my grumpiness. "Now get up, have a shower, I'm taking you to hospital."

But I could feel my eyes start to close again.

"Andrea" and they snapped back open again. "I'm serious, do I have to pick you up and put you in the shower myself?"

I know he was getting angry with me, because he only calls me Andrea when I'm in trouble. I couldn't help it though. I just wanted to be left alone to sleep. I did not want to have a shower, I did not want to go to the hospital, I did not want my temperature taken.

"ok ok ok..." I mumbled and rolled myself up to a sitting position with my legs hanging over the edge of the bed. I stared at the bathroom door, but nothing would come into focus, and my body didn't want to move. I began to feel lightheaded, not entirely dizzy, but stable enough to stand up.

"OK, I'm up."

But I could feel my body sway and start to relax, ready to slump back down onto the pillow, and I was already panting like I'd run the quarter mile.

'Focus girl' I shouted inside my head and leaned forward

forcing my legs to take my body weight while at the same time leaning against the door to the bathroom and attempting to take some deep breaths.

Now I'm the one who was getting angry with myself. My head felt like it was full of cotton wool, and my lungs were starving for oxygen. I felt not just drunk but, absolutely and totally plastered. I had to totally rely on Mick to help me shower, dry off, and get dressed, and even then, we had to take regular breaks for me to catch my breath again.

All I wanted to do was sleep and yet somehow, I managed to stumble through this process, allowing Mick to guide me exhausted but clean, into the front seat of the car.

'Mmm, the warmth of the sun through the windscreen is so nice.' I could feel it soak through my skin and reach the cold deep inside. Maybe I could just stay here in the car. 'Why am I here again? Oh, that's right ... Mick reckons I'm sick and have to go to the hospital, but he's wrong.' I wasn't sick, under my absolute tiredness I knew Mick was wrong and he was just worrying over nothing. It's a well-known fact that chemo patients do get very tired very quickly and require a lot more sleep.

"Babe, wake up." I opened my eyes just a small amount to see what all the fuss was about, only to be confronted with a sea of people running down the middle of Hay Street.

"What's going on?" I managed to mumble, not being able to comprehend the situation.

"It's the City to Surf fun run," Mick sounded exasperated. "They've got all the streets blocked off and I can't get through."

"Did you try going around?" I asked in the most unhelpful way.

"Of course, and I told them I need to get through. But they won't let anyone through." Even though I was barely comprehending the situation, I could hear in his voice that Mick was getting very agitated about how we were going to get to the hospital on the other side of the fun run.

"Just get on the freeway south." There are some things my brain is capable of, even when it's not fully functioning. "Get off at Canning Highway. Then get back onto freeway north and get off on Mounts Bay Road."

"OK" Mick sighed in frustration but turned the car back towards the freeway. "Stay with me babe, I might need directions."

It might have been the long way around, but it worked. The freeway passed over all the runners without a single one of them being aware Mick was in a desperate state to get me admitted into hospital.

With a quick flash of my chemo VIP card, Mick had me in my own room in emergency surrounded by a collection of doctors and nurses. With a needle in my arm and oxygen mask in place, I immediately started to feel better. Not get up and run around better, but enough to admit that Mick was right after all. I was pretty sick. As I started to doze off, I could see Mick looking at me in a way I'd never seen before.

"What?" I whispered.

"Nothing, just making sure you're not sooking," he

answered back. I could see it was more than that, but I didn't have the energy left to find out. The sounds of the hospital merged together into a dull hum, lulling me back to sleep. "I'll be OK. I'll be better after I've had a good night's sleep," I could hear myself mumble.

"Good morning, would you like some breakfast?" The tea lady was standing next to my bed. My eyes snapped open. I was on the hospital ward. Wow, that was quick. How did I get here? Last, I remember I was in emergency with Mick.

"You must have come in yesterday, as I don't have a breakfast order for you," she said. "So, what would you like?"

Yesterday? Breakfast? How long did I sleep? Mind you, it must have been a great sleep, because I felt so much better already.

"D.. u ..." where did my voice go. Uhummmm. I cleared my throat and pulled the oxygen mask off. "Do you have coco pops?" I managed to croak out some words. I couldn't believe how hungry I was.

"Of course we do," the lovely tea lady smiled a huge smile, almost laughing. "You chemo ladies are all the same, you really love your coco pops don't you." And with that she reached into her cart and came out with a breakfast tray.

"Hey, you're awake," a young nurse bounced into the shared ward. "And you've had breakfast too. That's fantastic. How are you feeling this morning?"

"Pretty good actually. A little dizzy when I sat up to eat, and still breathless." I picked up on her cheerfulness. "I'd love a shower though." I started to make moves towards getting out of bed. Woooo. A wave of dizziness came over me as I sat forward, and I struggled to breathe again.

"Oh no you don't young lady," she mock scolded, waggling her finger at me. "You are much too sick to be getting up. I'll come back soon with some fresh sheets and a sponge bath. And you will keep that oxygen mask on."

Really? A sponge bath? And the oxygen mask was so annoying to wear. The full-on mask isn't just like the little nose tubes. This thing was covering my nose and mouth, actually forcing oxygen down my lungs. And on top of that, have you ever tried to get your glasses to sit properly when you have a mask on? Trust me, it's near on impossible. So, I'm in a mood and starting to feel like an indignant child.

'Just you wait,' I thought defiantly, 'As soon as I get my head together, I'm going for a shower.'

O-oh ... 'Good morning bladder.' My bladder had woken up and it became more insistent that I did something about it. I considered the option of sneaking off to the toilet without the nurse noticing. After all, I only needed to get there, sit, rest, catch my breath.

"What are you doing?"

Oops, I was sprung, and she wasn't mock scolding me this time. "I was serious about you staying in bed with your oxygen."

"But I need to go to the toilet," I whispered. Embarrassed at the fact that I actually had to announce it out loud.

"Then I'll get you a pan," she was all business.

Oh, the absolute indignity of it all. Sure, she closed the curtains around my bed, but I knew that they knew what I was doing, and there would be no mistaking that sound once I actually did something.

"Still nothing?" she popped her head through the curtain quite some time later to check if I'd made pee pee yet.

"Nope," I said, partially embarrassed at the whole experience of having to pee in bed, and partially embarrassed that I'd delayed her schedule this morning by not being able to pee pee in bed.

"You must have a shy bladder. It happens." She took the pan away, unrolled a huge green hose attached to the oxygen outlet and helped me sit up.

"We'll go together, and we will go slowly," she announced.

'So, I have to take her with me? Really?' Now I was even more embarrassed.

I carefully stood up next to the bed, immediately starting to sway. I admitted to myself that maybe I did need some help, as we did the slowest ever three-legged race to the toilet, all the time taking deep breaths of oxygen as it was pumped through the hose and into my infected lungs.

"Just buzz when you're done, and I'll help you back to bed."

Thankfully once seated I did get some privacy. I was also definitely going to buzz when I had finished, as the short walk had worn me out, causing me to rely on the oxygen mask connected to the hose which wound its way under the door and all the way back to my bed.

"Ahhhhhh" and my bladder also showed its appreciation and lost its shyness.

Chapter 14
I'm Not Ready Yet

When you're lying awake, unable to sleep in the middle of the night, you hear a lot of things out of the darkened depths of the hospital wards. Some that you don't want to hear, and some that you probably shouldn't.

In the wee hours when she thought no-one was paying any attention, the very prim and proper lady in the bed across from me during one of my many stays, would quietly sneak out of bed, pull the curtains closed around her, and switch her TV over to Wrestle Mania. I would listen as she quietly cracked open her snack draw and very enthusiastically cheer whispered for her favourite wrestler. When I mentioned this to her one morning after such an event, she categorically denied that she would watch anything so barbaric, but that very night she again went through the same ritual. I just had to smile at the knowledge that everyone has an out to help them through the tough times, and sometimes that out is a little different

… like me and my drag racing.

There are other times, when lying awake, all you hear are the sounds of sadness and pain. Often, it's muffled crying or moaning, grunts and sighs, but there was one particular evening that not only brought tears to my eyes but crushed my soul. I could hear a lady's crying resonating up the hospital corridor to my ward. I didn't think it was specifically of sadness or even of pain, but then perhaps it was of both combined and more, because in between her sobs, she was begging the nurses to let her go. She simply did not want to fight any longer. It crushed me so much to hear this sad plea to be allowed to die, wondering how bad it had got, to make her want to give up. Unsure of how to handle my own emotion to what I'd heard, I simply rolled over in my own bed and quietly cried, hoping that I would never learn what that point was.

But you don't always get to make that choice. Sometimes it sneaks up on you without warning, and before you know it, you're kicking and screaming and coming to the true realisation of how short and precious life actually is.

I don't really know what caused me to wake up, but all of a sudden my eyes were as open as they could possibly be staring at the ceiling of a darkened hospital room, my body stretched out straight and stiff trying to open the airways to my lungs in hope that I could force more oxygen in. There was air going in and out, and the mask over my nose and mouth was doing its job to push clean oxygen down my lungs, but still I felt like I was suffocating.

Kicking off the blankets and struggling to sit up I tried to call out for help, but the words only came out as exhaled air without enough volume to grab even the attention of the other sleeping patients in my ward. My lungs were overruling my voice box, they wanted oxygen.

As I could feel the panic starting to build, I ignored the fact that there was cold air coming out of my mask and decided I'd probably just become tangled up in my air hose causing it to stop supplying me with much needed oxygen. You know how it is when you're watering the garden and give a pull on the hose only to find the pressure drop off to nothing. I forced myself to calmly and carefully trace my fingers along the hose to look for the kink that I was sure I would find, but as my fingers moved faster and faster with the panic of not finding any kinks, my breathing became more erratic as my lungs continued to scream for oxygen.

Tossing the hose aside and reaching for the emergency call button tucked under my pillow I pressed with enough force to turn my thumb white, as if the additional effort would somehow be replicated in the nurses' station alarm.

And somehow it worked. Somehow, she knew it was an urgent call. Because somehow while I was sitting on the end of my hospital bed trying to gasp every molecule of oxygen from that mask, that emergency button sent me a night angel in sensible shoes.

"Can't …. breathe …." I gasp.

She cranks the oxygen level up to max and I can feel the chill of it forcing its way through my nostrils and down the back of my throat, but I still feel like I'm drowning. Even though I'm taking huge gulps of air nothing is working. The room was dark before, but it now seems even darker around the edges, and my skin is starting to feel very cold. The only thing I can hear is my own heart thumping through my ears, but slowly the gentlest calm voice works its way through my panic. She is sitting on the bed with me, her hand rhythmically rubbing my back, and whispering in the calmest of all voices ... "breath slowly, count your breaths."

While I gasp and swallow, trying to capture everything I can, thinking that this is the end, I can hear her calm voice drifting in from a distance, but still it doesn't seem quite real. I'm still panicking. This is it. Is this how I go? But I'm not ready. I still have too much to do.

And that calm voice is there in the distance still, getting stronger, starting to take over my own thoughts. "breath slowly, count your breaths." And the rhythm of her hand rubbing my back is like I'm meditating.

I wanted to breath, I wanted to live, I wanted to put in every effort because there's too many things I want to accomplish. There's too much I still need to do.

"I'M NOT READY YET," while I am screaming this inside my head, I can feel my body relaxing.

As I relax the panic is lifting, and as the panic lifts I can feel the oxygen finally reaching my lungs. The dark edges around the world are starting to let in the soft night lights from the hospital corridor. The thumping in my ears begins to slow as I hear the sounds of the hospital around me return.

My eyes are closing with relief and weariness, I am exhausted. I can feel the cool oxygen being forced through the mask and down into my lungs, as my night angel gently lowers me back down onto the pile of pillows on my hospital bed. She doesn't speak but her kind eyes speak volumes.

I drift off in an exhausted sleep, without dreams, and with only one single thought ....

"Thank you."

Chapter 15
Visitor Tag ... You're It.

It doesn't matter where you're from or how you grew up, as a kid you would have played some version of a game called "Tag - You're It". Sometimes it would be a game with your friends, and at other times it would be the "you take the blame" game with your siblings when Mum and Dad caught you doing something you shouldn't. And still as an adult, at that moment when you're visiting your friend in hospital and someone else turns up, you can't help but utter the words "we won't crowd you" ... Tag - You're It. The other phrase muttered in hospital rooms is always, "We won't stay long, you need your rest." So even if you have a long list of friends and family popping by, it still does little to alleviate the boredom.

I'm BORED, I'm BORED. With all the drugs they have me on I don't actually feel sick, I've totally forgotten what sleep is, give me half a chance and unplug me from all these tubes and I'll run laps around the hospital. I'm

BORED!!!! Talk to me, tell me stories, share the gossip. I'm BORED!!!!!

I have watched all the TV I can stand, I've read books, I've done puzzles until my eyes crossed over. I've drawn, coloured, checked my phone, listened to the radio, nibbled on snacks and stared out the window at the new hospital extensions being built.

I'm BORED!!!!! I'm BORED!!!!! Especially when confined to bed, there's absolutely nothing to do in hospital. It's so boring and all I really crave is human interaction. I would find myself eavesdropping on the nurses' conversations down the corridor as if it was a tv soap opera, and then joining in on my roomies family time even though I would have no idea who these people were.

At last, I can hear Mum and Dad, well, mostly just Mum, her voice carrying through the hospital corridor down to my room.

"Did Michael say which room she was in?"

I can't believe it, I have visitors. Yay, my day is improving.

I so much want to call out to them, but all that comes out is a hoarse whisper. "I'm in here… cough cough cough…" I might as well save my voice, as I see Dad's face peek through the doorway into my shared hospital room. But instead of seeing me, his caring eyes scan each of the four hospital beds without recognition and before I can wave for his attention, he disappears back into the corridor.

"Maria, are you sure he said room 5?"

Mum steps into my room, and I start to sit up excitedly,

ready to receive my visitors. The hours of boredom dragging my day out into long lengths separated only by meals, medication and blood tests, is about to be pleasantly interrupted.

But Mum also briefly glances at each bed before walking straight back out again.

"Perhaps we got the wrong room, or maybe they moved her," she says to Dad. "I'll go and double check at the nurses' station."

I am gutted. How could they not see me? I try to call out again ... "m u m ..." the hoarse whisper barely escapes my cracking lips, and unable to hear me she's already walking away.

I prop myself up into a better seating position on the pillows, wrap my silk scarf around my bald head, and switch the light on over my bed in anticipation of their return. Because they have to return. They're my parents. They'll realise their mistake and be back laughing about it in no time. Because how can a Mum and Dad not recognise their own daughter. That's just absurd.

"Andy," the ward nurse comes into my room and heads over to my bedside carrying a spare visitor chair from one of my neighbours. "You have some visitors." She's overly chirpy and all smiles as she motions for Mum and Dad to come closer, so I pick up on the smiles and remove my oxygen mask, forcing the biggest smile I can muster to cover my dry, grey, thin face. Sure, the smile is a little bit fake, but Mum and Dad look so gloomy. Their faces are drawn with concern and worry.

"Ahhh, we didn't see you hiding in the corner," Dad forces his own fake smile and continues with his 'Dad joke'. "Anyone would think you didn't want visitors."

They don't ask how I'm doing. In fact, most people don't ask you that when you're in hospital. I guess it's because if you're in hospital, you're obviously not doing very well. Or perhaps it's because they don't really want to know the details. I have been known to offer a little too much information. But because I can't get out and do anything else, it's really the only thing I have to talk about. I can talk your ear off about the blood tests, the medications, nurses' visits in the middle of the night and attempting to shower while simultaneously not getting your canular wet or flooding water into your oxygen mask. There were only a couple of people I could have these open conversations with, and Mum and Dad certainly weren't them.

Mick would pop in every day, sometimes even twice a day, with a bright "Hi honey, how you feeling today?" and he would actually wait and listen patiently while I told him in the greatest of details, all my exploits since I'd last seen him. He would then grab my chart off the end of the bed and read the nurse and doctor comments because he knew that I probably wouldn't tell him the whole truth if I wasn't doing too well. He then wouldn't force unnecessary conversation realising that all I wanted was company, so he would pull up the easy chair beside my bed, switch on some news or sport on the TV and we would watch wordlessly together until he was ready to go, or I was drifting off to sleep.

"Andy, I have a couple of new shirts for you," Mum started unpacking the Target bags on the end of my bed, by way of avoiding any medical chatter from me. Mum rarely visited without gifts of some kind. Because it had been a particularly quiet day for visitors, she had the attention of everyone in the room, including our nurse. Sharing visitors is one of the bonuses for being in a shared room.

"Wow, I really love that checked shirt," mentioned Mrs Crafty from across the room. I don't know how long she'd been here, but the quilt she was knitting was almost finished, making her side of the room look very homely.

Mum picked up the shirt in question and took it over to Mrs Crafty's bedside. "Would you like me to get you one?" Mum asked, her mood picking up at the thought of being able to help someone else out.

"Oh no… you don't have to do that," Mrs Crafty was obviously embarrassed at a stranger's open offer to purchase a shirt for her.

"It's no bother at all," Mum folded the shirt back up again. No argument, the conversation was over. What Mum says is final. And true to her word, Mum was back the very next day with the same style shirt, neatly folded up with its price tag removed, in its Target shopping bag.

Chapter 16
My New Best Friend

When you're a little kid, making friends is really easy.

"I like black jellybeans."
"Wow, so do I."
"Cool, then we can be friends. Do you like brussel sprouts?"
"urgh, spew"
"Me neither, we can be best friends."
"Julie likes riding her bike lots, like me."
"I don't have a bike."
"Oh, Julie will be my best friend then."
"OK"

But somewhere between play dates and hitting the workforce I became a "grown up", took on "responsibilities", and became more aware, which made making friends more complicated. There is no reason why making friends shouldn't be easy, other than we let our emotions get too tangled up and forget that friends are someone to have a good time with. Being stuck on the cancer floor in hospital, starved for entertainment and mostly confined to my bed, making friends became easy again.

Well, at least with the other three people and the plethora of nurses, orderlies and cleaning staff who make the mistake of wandering too close to my bed and actually making eye contact. The longer I'm medically incarcerated the more people I am willing to chat with and the less fussy I became about making new friends.

I had been stuck in hospital for a week and even though my roomies were quite a bit older than me, they were extremely entertaining, and at times very comforting. Having been in a single room before, I've always preferred the option of a shared room, even if it does mean getting a more interrupted sleep.

In the bed directly across from me was Mrs Wheels, so nicknamed due to the fact she was unable to walk or even get out of bed without the aid of lifting equipment. She was a very patient lady who had to notify the nurse each time she needed to "go". After a sometimes-considerable wait for the orderly to come with the lifting thing, that actually resembles an engine hoist, she would be picked up from the bed and set down into a toilet seat wheelchair. She was then wheeled into the toilet and the process was then reversed to get her back into bed. She was not an exceptionally large lady, but new safety working practices prevented nurses and orderlies from lifting her in and out of the chair without the hoist.

Each time her lovely hubby turned up; he went straight to the nurses to arrange for Mrs Wheels to be put into a chair so he could take her for a walk to the local park. Each time they come back; they'd be giggling like teenage love birds that had been up to no good.

One particular day, Mrs Wheels, due to some new medication she'd been put on, just couldn't wait to "go". I watched her ring, and ring, and ring the buzzer getting more and more agitated as no-one answered her call. On seeing Mrs Wheels' agitation, myself and the other ladies in the ward decided to ring our buzzers on behalf of Mrs Wheels.

Great panic ensued throughout the nurses' station when all four buzzers kept sounding off at regular intervals.

"What's happening, what's the emergency," three nurses rushed into our room expecting a catastrophe.

"Mrs Wheels needs to 'go' REAL BAD," I piped up.
"Yes, we saw her buzz, but you other girls buzzing won't make us respond any quicker," one of the nurses scolded us as she went around the beds and reset all the buzzers.

We all smiled knowingly at each other, as we had got the response we wanted. The lifting machine was on its way and Mrs Wheels would be able to retain her dignity by going to the toilet.

The curtains swished closed and we listened to the orderlies fussing over Mrs Wheels, until we heard her cry, "It's too late, bring a pan."
"It's OK, Mrs Wheels, we'll get you in the chair shortly," responded the orderly.
"No, I'm telling you it's too late," she complained starting to sound a little panicky.

We could see the hoist moving over to the wheelchair and imagined her suspended and swinging without knickers, ready to land on the chair.

WHOOOOOOOSHTHWAT

"I told you," Mrs Wheels sobbed and cried.
As if the total indignity of having to wait for the nurse, then being suspended in this hoist wasn't enough, she had just released an explosive poop covering everything in a 3-meter radius.

"I told you, I told you," she kept crying as the nurse rushed out and closed our curtains so they could open hers for the big clean up.

"I'm so sorry," she kept sobbing.

After Mrs Wheels was cleaned up and returned to her bed, our curtains were drawn back, but Mrs Wheels curtain stayed drawn. She was embarrassed and needed some privacy.

Ms Prim in the bed next to Mrs. Wheels, looked totally disgusted and horrified at the whole experience. I've seen her in the waiting room down in oncology before, dressed to perfection with loads of make-up on and her nails so perfectly manicured, each to an exact length that it makes me wonder if they are fake.

But when she thinks no-one is watching in the middle of the night, she sits up in bed with her floral and lace high neck nightgown on, her wig firmly in place, with a cup of tea and watches Wrestle Mania on the TV.

Madame Wanderer shuffling into the room from

somewhere else on the ward was the perfect way to break the tension in the room.

"Got any ciggies?" her old raspy voice whispered as she approached each bed in turn.

Mick has often been approached by this dear old lady on his regular visiting time straight after work.

"Come along now Madame," the nurse gently guided her out of the room as if redirecting a sleepwalker.

"You know you are not allowed to smoke, that's why you have patches."

"Well I never," Mrs Chatterbox piped up in the bed next to mine.

"They really need to control their patients and not let them wander about annoying everyone else."

Her hubby remained quiet during his usual visit to deliver a fresh nightgown, book or slippers only to be informed it's the wrong one. Since no-one commented, she turned her attention to Mr Chatterbox, filling him in on the day's activities at the hospital and complaining they've given her the wrong treatment, how she should be on this diet, and that she should have a private room.

Thankfully, I only had to deal with the incessant chatter and complaining from her for a couple of days. I had never seen the nurses clean out a bed so quickly as when they got the notification from the doctor that Mrs. Chatterbox was being sent home.

"But I haven't had my lunch yet, and I've ordered my lunch," she protested loudly, crossing her arms over her chest. It was only 10am. Why would she even want to hang around for hospital food when she could go home?

"I'll take her discharge papers if she doesn't want them," I joked with the nurse when she came over my side of the room, both of us silently giggling at the silliness of it all.

"We have to make the bed ready for another patient," the head nurse had come in to see what all the fuss was about.

"You can sit in the chair and wait for your lunch if you like, but I need you out of the bed."

I had never seen someone so annoyed at being told to go home. She packed up all her stuff, spent an hour in the bathroom getting dolled up ready to go home, and then sat with her bags by the chair and not only defiantly waited for her lunch but also made hubby wait too.

The nurses worked around them, stripping the bed and remaking it ready for the next cancer patient.

Lisa was wheeled in, nurse by her side, and her hubby close behind carrying her "it holds everything I might ever possibly need" handbag.

Wow, at last, someone my own age. And she doesn't look sick either, apart from the beanie covering up her bald patches on her head. Lisa sat on the bed and hubby looked around to find their visitor chair taken by Mrs Chatterbox.

He looked confused. 'Why is this lady sitting there?'
"She won't leave until she's had her lunch," I said.
He looked at me as though I was out of my mind.
"But feel free to use my chair. My hubby won't be in until after work."

He took the chair, and stayed to settle his wife in. I couldn't wait for Mick's regular visit after work so I could fill him in on the day's events.

Rattle, rattle, rattle, I could hear the tea trolley doing it's rounds through the wards.

'Mmmm, lunch time', my tummy growled at me. It was not a coincidence that the only time I was super hungry was when I was in hospital. The doctors not only prescribed loads of antibiotics to kill all the bugs, they also prescribed steroids, which unfortunately for my once size 8 figure, made me want to eat all the time.

"Hi, you're new," the tea lady plopped a lunch tray on Lisa's trolley.

"Have a quick look and see if you like it, if not, I'll grab you something else." And she turned to hand out other lunch trays from the tea trolley.

"That's my lunch," Mrs Chatterbox jumped up from her seat and grabbed the tray off Lisa's trolley. The tea lady immediately took it back off her.

"No, you have been discharged. Only patients with beds get lunch," she retorted.

Lisa and her hubby just sat there totally gob smacked at the behaviour of this older woman while Mrs Chatterbox's hubby sat across the room quietly, trying to shrink into his own shadow.

"I ordered that lunch, and I'm not leaving until I receive it," Mrs Chatterbox answered back.

At which time the on-duty nurse walked into the ward, looked at the tea lady with sympathy.

"Just let her have it and give Lisa a fresh lunch."

"Hmpf," a self-satisfied sound came from Mrs Chatterbox as she grabbed the lunch tray from the tea lady and settled down to eat it. What delicacy did she fight so hard for? Her lunch consisted of some greyish looking lumps in gravy with white powdered mash on the side, followed by some jiggly yellowish pudding for dessert.

"What on earth was that all about?" Lisa looked over at me with bright eyes full of laughter and mischief, once Mrs Chatterbox had finally finished her lunch and gone home with her mousey hubby in tow.

"I'm not sure you would believe me if I told you," I giggled back. I could see we were going to get along. She was going to be my new best friend.

Chapter 17
What's on the Menu?

It turns out that the only reason I found myself hugging the porcelain bus in the middle of the night after my first chemo was because I hadn't understood the instructions and hadn't taken enough anti-nausea medication BEFORE chemo. That is certainly not a mistake I repeated. The medication might have made me feel like I was in the middle of the Sahara without a drink in sight, and gave me a bone crushing headache, but at least it kept my dinner down.

While on the subject of dinner, I did discover that my taste buds had now gone on holiday with my brain and left me with a cheap metallic robot impersonator in their place. I say metallic because it's the closest thing I can find to describe the taste of ... well, everything, although I'm not sure that it's a totally accurate description of the taste, or lack of. If you'd like to try that flavour for yourself, try licking a freshly buffed sheet of stainless steel. So now

I, the lover of food, eater of anything, had absolutely no interest in food, and don't even get me started on the gallons of water that I was also supposed to be drinking every day to prevent the dehydration that the chemo was causing.

Poor Mick had been cooking his giant heart out trying to find something that I could eat, but when you have no appetite and the look, smell and especially taste of food holds absolutely no interest, it's very hard to be a grateful dinner guest.

"So dinner for zee chef iz," Mick pranced over to the table, tea towel draped over his arm, and with his best French waiter flourish put his plate on the table. "Iz a medyum rib ay stek, wiz mash potato, und a tomato n onion salat wiz a swish ov Italian dressig."

I was sitting at the table, freshly showered and in my pj's, sucking on an icy pole. I was smiling but not laughing. Don't get me wrong, I was rolling on the floor laughing on the inside, but it had been a long time since I'd laughed out loud. It's not that I had lost my sense of humour, I was just simply tired all the time, and laughing required energy I would save up - to do stuff like shower and eat.

"Und fer Madam," he came back to the table with my plate. "Now zat she as finished her icey-pole aperitif to prepare er stomach and taste buds for this gastronomic delight, I present you wiz," and he put my plate in front of me. "lightly grilled fish wiz no seasoning or flavour, some boring salad without any zest and an egg, unsalted."

Mick whisked the tea towel off his arm, bowed and said, "bon appetit."

And with that he sat at the table and got stuck into his own meal. I stared at mine, willing my stomach to behave, but suddenly felt too tired and uninterested to put anything in my mouth.

We had spent some time experimenting with different foods, finally coming to an agreement with my taste buds that fish and eggs still tasted like fish and eggs. That is fish AND eggs, not fish eggs. A cup of warm Cinnamon and Apple tea or an icey-pole before dinner was able to trick my stomach into eating a little.

I am so lucky to have a brother-in-law who just happens to live in Shark Bay and actually work out on the water every day.

"It's my mission to keep you stocked up with quality fresh fish," he proudly stated on his last visit down to Perth with an esky full of Blue Bone fillets.

"This little lot was hard work, so you'd better enjoy them," he chuckled. He swore he slaved over a fishing rod for weeks to keep me in stock, but I know he also enjoyed it. It was simple acts like this from friends and family that made the treatment so much easier, not just on me, but also on Mick, who now didn't have to worry about what to feed me.

Just as I was getting used to my own brand of "chemo food" and even considered starting up a recipe book called 'what you can get to the stomach without the taste buds noticing', I got to taste the cuisine of the experts. Now you may think my choice of food was something even a starving baby in a third world country would reject, and I would have agreed with you, until I discovered that I had been one-upped by the hospital kitchen staff and their special meals for the cancer ward.

With my many vacations in hospital, where I reckon Mick was only sending me so he could have a rest, because I swear I wasn't really sick, I discovered that there is a hierarchical food appreciation system based on the patient's illness, longevity of stay and chances of leaving. Being that most of us patients on the cancer ward didn't believe we were even close to being as sick as they actually were, and therefore quite chatty to any and all staff, we were often given dispensation when it came to choosing our meals. Sure, you still have to put in your menu card with all the boxes ticked but have a quiet chat to the tea lady when she comes around, and you'll find there's a few extras available that aren't on the menu. For example, if you mention that just a fruit platter would be nice for lunch, out comes the special vegetarian menu card, with a whole swag of additional choices.

Before I was introduced to the system by Mrs Crafty, who had been laid up for long enough to have almost completed her knitted bedspread, I found the hospital meals to be rather lacking.

It's not that they were lacking so much in flavour, since I had already dispensed with the idea of ever being able to correctly identify the difference between the green jellybean and the black one, but rather in warmth and appearance. Everything needed to be the exact same temperature, regardless of whether it was ice cream or sausages and mash, and it also needed to be the same colour.

My uncle used to work as a baker making buns for a popular burger place, and he said they had an actual colour chart to check the buns all looked the same. I reckon the hospital kitchen has a similar chart, but it consists of 50 shades of grey.

The menu card would arrive on the breakfast tray, allowing you to peruse through your choices over your first meal of the day, provided you hadn't been banished onto a special diet like poor Mrs B&B. Normally the busy owner of a lovely Bed & Breakfast up in the hills, she was banished to receive her meals as liquid via a tube through her nose and direct to her stomach. After seeing her experience with hospital cuisine, I decided I would be more thankful that at least I was able to feed myself and have a choice of food.

"Oh wow, lunch sounds wonderful," Lisa, my new hospital room mate exclaimed on receiving her menu card on the breakfast tray.

"I can't decide if I should order the 'Beef Stroganoff mixed with onions, mushrooms, sour cream, and herbs, served over a bed of lightly whipped baby potatoes and serving of steamed crispy in season vegetables' or the 'The fresh fish pie topped with lightly whipped baby potatoes and encrusted with golden toasted breadcrumbs served with steamed crispy in season vegetables.'"

Even with my lack of taste buds and the fact I'd already been subjected to this lavish food for the past week, my mouth was watering, so I could totally understand Lisa's delight as a newbie to this menu. But I also knew how bitterly disappointed she would be when the food finally arrived, and she realised that the menu had been designed by an overzealous graphic designer with little or no consultation with the kitchen staff.

"I hate to disappoint," I carefully broached the subject of inedible food with my new best friend, "but it won't even look like what they've described, let alone taste like it."

"But they can't really get a stroganoff that wrong, can they?" she asked me wistfully.

I could see the pleading in her eyes for some really nice food. I guess the antibiotics and steroids were kicking in and making her hungry.

"You'd be surprised. I suggest going for the absolute basic, but if you wanna give it a go, don't say you haven't been warned." I finished off my cocopops, an absolute staple of many chemo patients, and filled out my card for the next three meals.

"Cold meat salad for me with a fruit platter on the side with some cheese and crackers that I can save for later. You really can't muck it up."

Lisa gave me a determined look, "I'm going for the stroganoff, and for dessert I'll have the rice pudding." I watched with a wry smile as she filled out the card while nibbling on a piece of cold toast covered with freeze dried whipped yellow something and a red jelly like topping.

Needless to say, when dinner arrived, Lisa was bitterly disappointed with her canned meat with gravy, powdered mash and over cooked frozen veg. But apparently the rice pudding was quite nice. I'll have to give it a go next time.

After my first stay in hospital, I soon realised that a simple change in medication – usually the addition of steroids after an infection – quickly changed my interest in food, and sometimes even allowed the tastebuds to make a brief return.

Following one of these medication changes, and on one of my particularly good days at home, I decided to treat Mick to a meal fit for a king. Choosing to make a change from our regular fish diet, I instead headed off to renew my friendship with the local butcher and get some nice big, freshly cut, tender steaks for my man. Then I headed off to the fresh veggie shop for some giant field mushrooms, fresh beans and carrots and baby potatoes. Real ones, not the powdered or frozen stuff you get at the hospital.

I was so excited. Not only did I have an appetite and interest in food, but I also had the energy to cook a full meal. Just to make sure, I had a bit of a nap after going shopping, as I knew that it could be short lived if I didn't pace myself.

"Woof woof woof" the dogs went running for the front door, and I heard Mick's car door slam closed. He was home from work. So, I was up off the couch and started to buzz about the kitchen, getting everything ready.

"Wow, feeling good?" Mick asked as he dumped his lunch box on the counter and grabbed a cold beer from the fridge.

"You have no idea," I beamed back at him. "AND I feel hungry too."

There was no need to mention that I had taken a nap to

make sure I'd be up for the job. It was enough that I felt great and had energy to burn. Hopefully I wouldn't burn out too quickly.

"Cool, do I have time for a shower before dinner?"

"You sure do babe," I smiled back, and started to sing as I put the potatoes on the boil.

"So, dinner for zee chef iz," I pranced over to the table, tea towel draped over my arm, copying Mick's impersonation of a French waiter, and put his plate on the table. "Iz a medium rib ay stek, wiz baby potato, und lightly steamed freshly picked vegetables."

I rushed back to the kitchen and got my plate piled high with exactly the same.

"You dag, you," Mick laughed at me and raised his beer to my little glass of wine.

"Cheers to the good days."

It was the perfect dinner. The steak was the perfect shade of pink inside, tender and juicy. The potatoes were nice and creamy, and the vegies still had that little bit of crunch. It might be difficult to believe, but I ate every single thing on my very full plate.

Oh boy, sitting back after eating all that I started to feel a little sick, but it was a nice kinda sick, the "I ate too much" kind of feeling.

It was so nice to feel a little bit normal again.

Chapter 18
Bum Fluff

Oh wow, my hair is growing back. I can see it; I can feel it. I'm so excited that soon I'll have hair again. I wonder how long it will take to fully cover my head, I wonder what colour it will be, I wonder if it's going to be curly like everyone else seems to have after chemo.

"Are you sure?" Mick asks me trying to be positive but letting on by way of peering extremely closely at my head, that he's more than just a little concerned for my sanity.

"I can't see anything," my sister lets me know.

"Surely, it's a bit early, isn't it?" Mum asks, looking a little closer but not expecting to find any new follicles. "You're still doing chemo."

"It is! IT IS!!!!!" I claim bold and loud and almost stamping my feet, like a whining child who's not getting their own way. "You're just not looking hard enough." I gently run my hand over the top of my head and feel that reassuring softness that wasn't there only a matter of weeks ago.

It's just a little bit of white fuzz that's not only covering my head but also the entirety of the rest of my body, and I have to stand in the sunlight to be able to see anything, but it's definitely starting to grow. I've been looking at this bald shiny head for months, so I should know. I want to keep touching it because it's so soft like velvet, but I'm afraid that if I do, I might rub it all away. But I still can't help touching it.

I might not have finished my chemo treatment yet, but Dr Geeza did say that while this last drug that they've got me on might be toxic to the cancer, my body and my general wellbeing, it's not toxic to hair growth, so I could expect it to start coming back. I'm so excited about the prospect of having hair again, but seriously disappointed that no-one else is sharing in my joy.

I have a solution. Everyone just needs to see my head in the right light. So, I choose a particularly sunny day, spikey up my not even millimetre long hair - very carefully - grab up my camera and start taking selfies.

AARRRRCHOOOOOOOO!

Dam it's bright out here. I'm one of those people who sneeze in bright light, even if you turn the bedroom light on in the middle of the night, you'll get not just one, but a nice set of three sneezes from me. It's a real and hereditary thing called "Archoo Syndrome." So, with still no eyelashes to protect my additionally chemo sensitive eyes I look like I'm crying in every photo. Why didn't my eyelashes grow back first? Surely that would make more sense.

Did you know that different parts of the body have their own hair growth timeline? Well you probably did, but did you know that different parts of your head even have their own growth timeline? While it fell out in patches, I was very surprised to see that it was also growing back in patches. Not really obvious patches like when it fell out, and certainly not noticeable yet but as it got longer, I could see the front had a much slower growth rate to the back.

Aim, smile, CLICK.

Nope can't see any hair in that shot. Isn't digital photography amazing? I can't see anything on the camera viewfinder so I head back inside to rest my eyes and plug the camera into the computer so I can see the result on the big screen. How frustrating, nothing is showing up. Maybe if I get the sun shining on my head from behind, so back out into the back yard I go. I can't do this out the front, as I really don't need to be added entertainment for the neighbours.

As frustrating as it is, I am absolutely determined to record this momentous occasion, and prove to everyone that there is definitely hair there. I don't know what makes me think that I can capture on film what they can't see with their own eyes, but I'm not going to give up.

Avey and Peppa look at me with amusement, with heads cocked to one side as if to say, "whatcha doing Mum?" Avey even sniffs closely at my head on a couple of occasions, attempting to see for herself what all the fuss is about. 'Seriously Mum, I have more hair on my belly.'

It doesn't take long before they both decide taking photos of my hair growth is boring, and the photos would be much more interesting if there were dogs in them.

Before long I have hundreds of photos of every angle of the top of my head with the odd dog nose, ears and tongue licking my ears thrown in for good measure. And my eyes are streaming so much now from all the sunshine, that I can't see what I'm taking photos of anymore. Time to call it quits and use the zoom, enhance and sharpen feature on Photoshop. There will definitely be one photo in that mix that is worthy of posting on Facebook with pride. Facebook friends will always support and back you up ... won't they? After all, you need to be positive and nice to people fighting cancer. It's in the friend rule book.

Unfortunately, if there was such a book, I don't think any of my friends read it. It might sound harsh, but the reality of it is, that's why we're friends in the first place. I come from the school of "don't ask if you don't want to know the truth." So, I tend to accumulate friends who have the same mindset. This also means that if you're looking for false platitudes just to pick up your mood, they're a little hard to find. Not that it really matters. What's important is that I know my hair is growing back, even if no-one else can see it. They'll be able to see it soon enough.

My mind wanders back to the same thoughts every post chemo patient must have. I wonder how long it will take for my hair to grow back. I wonder what colour it will be? Will it stay white like the current fuzz? That would be cool. I wonder if it will be curly. I had very curly hair as a little kid, and heaps of ladies on the support groups talk about their previously straight hair coming back super curly. And what part of my body is going to get "real" hair first?

It sucks not having hair on my head, but there's some real bonuses to not having it anywhere else as well. NO SHAVING required. Yay. And considering I'm still going through treatment, and very prone to infections, I'm not supposed to shave or even wax anyway. So while I want my head hair back - the sooner the better please - I don't want my underarm or leg hair back. Can I please put in an order?

Sorry, but it doesn't work that way. Murphy's law says that all the hair you don't want will grow back first and really quickly and really noticeably, while all the hair you do want will take forever and then won't come back the way you want it. As humans we really are obsessed by our hair.

And then there's the hair that grows back where you didn't realise you had hair to begin with. Perhaps I am just naive, but I seriously didn't know you have little hairs down your throat, in your ears, and a few other places that aren't that obvious until there's none there anymore.

"Dr Geeza, I'm really worried about this cough I've developed." At Micks insistence, I bring up my constant dry hacking cough at my next oncology appointment. Even just talking about it causes me to cough in demonstration.

"Perhaps she's having another allergic reaction to the chemo?" Mick gives his well-considered opinion. With all the drugs I've been on, and all the reactions I've had, Mick should probably be given an honorary doctorate. Dr Mick, fully qualified to discuss in detail, any and all aspects of his wife's treatment and proffer opinions based on his ability to see through her tough exterior when something is wrong.

But Dr Geeza smiles in that off handed way he has, and even adds a little laugh to it.

"Your hair is growing back Andy, and that cough is just an irritation caused by the hairs in your throat growing back too."

"Oooooooooooh!" Mick and I both laugh with relief that it's nothing at all serious, and then simultaneously feel a little ashamed that we both know so little about our own anatomy that we didn't realise this ourselves.

"Don't feel embarrassed about not knowing, it's quite common. And because you were a smoker before you started treatment, you probably didn't have any there to begin with." Dr Geeza wasn't finished there either. He leaned forward over his desk towards me and lowered his voice as if he was sharing a well-kept secret.

"You might notice that it's a little easier to poo?"

Well, wasn't I getting an education! I shot Mick a quick glance to see if he had cottoned onto what Dr Geeza was talking about, but he still looked none the wiser. 'That's OK,' I thought, 'there's some stuff not everyone needs to know about, although I'm sure I'll still let Sue know, because that's just her kind of thing.' Everyone has at least one friend who likes to know all the information no matter how intimate the detail is , and then there is the other friend who is still just as supportive, but really only wants to know the nice stuff like how soft your new hair on your head is, or how they can take advantage of it for fundraising.

"I'm not sure if I'm feeling up to this breast cancer fundraiser," I complain over the phone to Suze. I've only just had my latest chemo, and I'm really feeling 'out of it'. "Seriously, I'm not going to be any fun for anyone."

"But you're one of the guests of honour," she replied. "It wouldn't be the same without you. Just come along for a little bit, and if you're not feeling up to it, we can prop you up in a corner."

"Sure, I can do that," I said. I didn't feel very confident about the whole thing, but there were going to be a lot of my friends and family there, so I thought I should at least try.

One thing I have learnt along the way, is that if you're not feeling the best, but you have to go out, you can "fake it until you make it". I still use this approach finding that once I'm there, wherever there is, I start to feel the vibe of the party and it improves my energy level. So I got out the makeup, and the brightest pink shirt I could find, donned my fancy dress long blonde wig, kindly donated by a publican friend who received it as a bizarre beer promotion and soldiered on to do my bit for the cancer fundraising campaign.

The wig didn't say on my head for long though. When you don't have a layer of hair between your skin and the wig netting it's just hot and irritating. The nice expensive wigs have a lovely lining, or you wear a soft skull cap, but this was a cheap promotional fancy dress wig, so it had to come off if I stood any chance of lasting the night.

"Can I feel your new hair fuzz? I've heard it's like a newborn baby's hair."

I cannot believe a total stranger at the pub where we are having the fundraiser is actually asking me this. It's like a total stranger asking a pregnant lady if they can feel the bump. But I guess we were being a little loud, and Roz and I had decided to do the rounds of the other patrons to see if we could get anymore donations in the tin.

"You can but you have to make a donation." Roz - Suze's sister - is on the ball with this one. She's a couple of months ahead of me in her treatment, having already finished her chemo and moved onto radiation, so her hair is well past the soft fluff stage and has moved onto the, 'I've just joined the army and got a crew cut' stage.

"Really?" I look at her incredulous at her brazenness. No-one is going to 'pay' to feel my hair. But even before I had decided that this was an absolutely insane idea, and that perhaps the radiation was messing with Roz's mind, the total stranger was opening his wallet.

"Sure," he said, stuffing a couple of not so small notes into the fundraising tin. Roz raised her newly grown back eyebrows at me and gave me a very cheeky grin. "Should we see if anyone else wants to pay to pat your head?"

"Really?" I asked incredulously again. "You got lucky with a fella who's had a bit too much to drink. No-one else will fall for that."

"What have we got to lose?" Roz put her arm around me, rattled the tin, and boldly lead me around the bar. "Make a donation towards breast cancer and Andy will let you feel her velvety soft new hair."

And believe it or not, Roz had them lining up with

donations at the ready, all wanting to pat my head. And to add extra credit, she was not accepting small donations either, as most of what I saw going into the tin was in the form of folding notes.

"Be gentle … don't rub too hard … let the next person have a go now … really, is that all you think it's worth? …" Roz was having a ball, while I just lowered my head for each pat, smiled at the platitudes, and allowed her to lead me around the pub with the quickly filling fundraising tin.

But just like with new babies the soft velvet fuzz doesn't last very long which is why Roz was able to turn it into such a successful fundraising activity so easily. And unfortunately, the pure white that I was desperately hoping to hang onto was being replaced just as quickly by harsh, very curly dark grey.

Don't get me wrong, I really do love having hair again, but it's so much work. I've almost become a bit blasé about having minimal hair for over a year. No straighteners, no curlers, no hairspray, no hairdressers, not even any shampoo or conditioner. Now I wake up and look in the mirror and it's wild and unruly curly mop on top with a bit flat patch on the back. I mean not just a little bit wavy; it now looks like I've had a perm.

I had to ditch the grey almost straight away though, feeling pretty drained and wrung out already by all the treatment, I just couldn't look at that old lady in the mirror anymore.

Back to the hairdresser I hadn't seen since she originally cut off all those lovely long locks of blonde hair in what seemed like another lifetime ago.

"Jamie Lee, I need you to do something with .... THIS..." I waved my hands over my grey, uneven, curly mop.

"I don't want to put any harsh chemicals on it yet," she said. "So, no blonde. How about a gentle rinse?"

So gone was the grey, to be replaced by a reddish brown, but what on earth was I supposed to do to manage these curls?

Step one, spray lightly all over with water. Step two, fluff up lightly with fingers. Step three, apply beanie carefully so as not to allow weird sticky uppy bits. Leave for about 1 hour before removing beanie and refluffing.

I should totally patent this idea. How many people out there have newly curly hair and have no idea that you can't use a hairdryer or a brush if you don't want to look like one of those over used toy hairstyling heads that were around when I was a little kid. Every now and then you see an old one in the toy section of the op shop with crazy permanent marker eyebrows in a state of perpetual surprise, blue eyeshadow and matted cotton wool hair that's gone beyond allowing any form of combing device through it.

But just like the soft fluff, the curls were also short lived. And just when I was getting used to them too.

Chapter 19
No More Chemo

No more chemo, no more chemo, no more chemo. I couldn't help but sing and dance. I was so excited. It was the last one. The last Friday had almost arrived, and I would get to put that great big red X on the calendar at last. I had to admit that there were a few times that I didn't think I was going to make it this far. But here it was, the very last time I will ever have to have that horrible poison pumped through my veins.
But this time it wouldn't be just me and Mick heading off for our usual hospital jaunt, this time I had a special couple of guests to help me celebrate. On Wednesday I headed out to the airport to pick up my biggest supporters, my bestie Sue and her daughter - my goddaughter - Lucy who had flown in from Paraburdoo to make sure that my last chemo didn't pass without a little bit of fanfare. Well, Sue wasn't just here for that, she had other things to do in Perth, but made sure she booked her trip to coincide with my celebration. The last time we'd seen each other

in person, because we had skyped quite a bit, was when she came to Perth to take me for my very first haircut and go hat shopping. With everything that had happened, it seemed like such a long time ago, but in reality, it had only been a few months. Isn't it odd how the more you do, and the more eventful time has been, the longer amount of time appears to have passed?

I stood at the bottom of the airport arrival escalators, scanning every person as they appeared at the top, and at the same time hopping from one foot to the other in excitement. Nope, that's not them, not them either, nope... where are they? Then just as the crowd of arrivals was starting to thin out, and I was starting to get a little worried that they hadn't made their plane, I saw Sue's smiley face appear at the top of the ride. My heart skipped a beat, and my tummy fluttered as I watched the excruciatingly slow escalator deliver my bestie to me.

"OMG OMG OMG," all three of us squealed and group hugged until it hurt. "OMG OMG OMG." We jumped around still holding each other and squealing, attracting quite a few glances from the other passengers around the airport.

"OK, let's grab our suitcases and hit the shops," Sue was on a mission for this visit. So, it was definitely a case of Midland shopping centre, look out, we're on our way.

"Where should we start?" Sue's eyes were huge like a kid in a candy shop once we got out of the car in the shopping centre carpark. She had a card full of savings and was ready to melt some plastic.

"How about we grab a trolley and just work our way from

one end of the shops to the other," I suggested, smiling at her eagerness. This was awesome, it had nothing to do with hospitals, doctors or treatment. It was all about getting some serious and well needed retail therapy done. If you saw the size of the shops at Paraburdoo, you would understand why Sue needed this outing and also why she was so excited. And buying stuff online was still a relatively new hit and miss experience, so there was no other option for someone living in a very small remote town, but to head to Perth once or twice a year with a big list.

We spent the rest of the day flitting from shop to shop, finally stumbling out to the car with two trolley loads full of goodies, sore feet, and red-hot bank card. Now you'd probably think with three girls heading off to the shops that we came home with loads of clothing but sadly I'll have to disappoint you. We in fact had among other things, bathmats, towels, a toaster, sheets, a couple of jars of pickles and yes, a few clothes for the very quickly growing, Miss Lucy.

"Phew, I reckon I could sleep for a week after that," I exclaimed, flopping back onto the couch once we'd finally made it home. Even though I was in the final phase of my chemo cycle, and I was feeling pretty good, I was still absolutely exhausted after so much running about. I'd forgotten how much energy going shopping all day could take out of you, and especially since I was very out of practice.

"Oh you should have let me know you were tired," Sue gave me a concerned look and Lucy sat next to me giving me a gentle hug as though she was worried that I would break.

"I'm fine," I said, returning Lucy's hug and trying to force away the look of tiredness on my face. "Don't stress. How often do I get a chance to go out and spend someone else's money? It was fun."

"Yeh, well, OK then." But she didn't look convinced.

Sue knew me too well and was pretty sure I had overdone it. "I will arrange take away for dinner tonight though, I don't want you making yourself sick."

"You've got a deal, because Lucy and I are making cupcakes tomorrow to share around the chemo ward at the hospital." I remembered the lady with the pink wig on my first day in the chemo rooms and smiled at Lucy who was just excited at the prospect of doing creative stuff with me. Painting, drawing, sewing, baking, decorating ... this was our thing. When they lived in Perth Sue would call me to help out with costumes, cakes and totally customised party decorations. We even made up our own party games. We were by no means experts, but everything was made with heaps of love and enthusiasm.

Just the thought of making a mess of icing, sprinkles and sparkles with these two ladies again made me start to feel better already. I could feel myself recharging but knew that I would have to actually relax for the rest of the evening if I was going to make it through another whole day.

"We have lots to do, so I'll need all my energy."

But no matter how much I might have needed to relax and sleep, I couldn't help but toss and turn all night. Part of the problem was because I was just over tired, but the other part was I was simply super excited. Excited that my bestie was in town, and excited - believe it or not - that my last chemo was only 1 day away.

I tried to sleep in, catching a few extra minutes here and there, cuddled up to the dogs, but eventually gave up and decided I could have a nap later if needed. There was a good chance I'd doze off in the chemo chair anyway once I was snuggled under that fresh warm blanket they give you.

"Well it looks like it's just us," I said to Avey and Peppa, wandering through the quiet house to put the kettle on for a coffee.

"Should we get these cupcakes made so they're ready to decorate when the girls get home from their chores?" I was of course speaking to my dogs, but the only response I received was a couple of heads tilted slightly as if to say, "Does that mean we can lick the bowl?"

"Righto then, breakfast, drugs, shower, check in the mirror to see if I have any visible hair yet, then let's get baking."

Sadly, there was still no real hair visible in the mirror.

"Oh wow," I heard Sue coming through the front door a couple of hours later with yet more shopping bags. I had no idea how she was going to fit everything in their suitcases for the trip home, but Sue wasn't only good at shopping, she was also a master of packing. "It smells amazing in here."

"Totally, Yummo," exclaimed Lucy, her eyes lighting up at

the sight of the three big trays of cupcakes cooling on the bench under the watchful eyes of two eager dogs.

"I thought you were going to wait until we got home though," Sue was scolding me in the way only a best friend can, for overdoing it again.

"I figured they would need time to cool," I explained, knowing that Sue would see through my semi lie, but she would also realise that I just needed to keep myself distracted. There was a lot going on in my head, and while I might have been excited about finishing chemo, I was also very nervous about the next stage of treatment. I'd heard a lot of horror stories about radiation.

"Now all that's left is the fun bit."

I opened up the big silver case filled full of cake decorating stuff that my sister and I have continually added to over several years of making cakes. Neither of us are professional, nor have we even done proper training, but we love to live in the belief that the Woman's Weekly cakes are as easy to make as they say they are. Sue and I started a tradition of making Lucy's birthday cake together each year, beginning with a great big bunch of balloons with liquorice strap ribbons, for her first birthday. Every year we have challenged ourselves to make something a little more exciting, and every year it would take a little more wine, a little more icing, and a lot more laughter. Lucy would be sent off to bed, the hubbies would sit a safe distance away from the kitchen, and Sue and I would pull out all the decorations, a picture from the magazine, and start with… "So how are we going to get this one to work?"

When Sue, Paul and Lucy moved up to Paraburdoo, I still made the flight up just before Lucy's birthday, with a suitcase full of cake mix and decorations. The flies and the heat added its own challenges, but it was a tradition not to be missed, and a great excuse for us girls to get together.

Unfortunately, this year was the first year I couldn't be there to make Lucy's cake, but I didn't want to mess with tradition. Lucy's Grandma, Vera, mentioned that she was heading up with Lucy's GranDad, John, from Perth to see Lucy for her birthday. We decided together that I could take my time to make some icing butterflies and flowers, and when she got to Paraburdoo, she could make the cupcakes.

It worked a treat. I took my time creating lots of intricate cake toppers, and carefully packaged them up in cotton wool and Tupperware so they would survive the long journey. Unfortunately, Sue can't handle touching cotton wool, so while she was excited to see the finished result when it arrived, she did let me have it for packing them up the way I did. We still laugh about it now.

"Oh, so cool Auntie Andy," Lucy immediately poked her head into the box of cake decorations that I'd opened on the kitchen table and started sorting through looking for pink, shiny and sparkles.
"Now remember they will all have pink icing, so just pull out the decorations suitable for pink cupcakes," I reminded her.

"Wow, Mum look. There's glitter that you can eat. And little flowers."

"Lucy, you remember this is Auntie Andy's special day,"

Sue reminded her over excited daughter who was pulling out everything pink, white or silver from the box, placing it on the plastic covered dining table.

"Don't stress Sue, let her have fun." I joined in picking out the readymade pink icing and a few tools to make decorating a little easier. "As long as I have cakes to hand out, I'm happy."

Sue grabbed up all the mini cupcakes from the kitchen and moved them to the middle of the dining table. I added the knife into icing mixture and declared, "Let's do this, and anything that falls on the floor is fair game for the dogs."

As if by invitation, we were immediately joined by Avey and Peppa, ready and willing to clean up any mess that made it to the floor. After all, that's one of the best reasons to have dogs isn't it?

"Oh my god," Mick exclaimed walking through the front door after several hours of decorating fun. "We've been attacked by the pink glitter fairies."

All three of us were covered in glitter and sparkles, with Lucy especially covered around her face, and in particular, the mouth. There were also pink and white balls all over the table, dribbles of pink icing covering most of the plastic tablecloth, and two very hyperactive dogs pretty impressed at their success in keeping the floor clean.

"Look how many we made Uncle Mick," Lucy was so proud. "And each one is totally different."

Mick followed her over to the kitchen bench where we had placed the cakes, ready to be packed up for the morning trip to the hospital.

"I made this one, and this one, and that one..." Lucy was so excited pointing out each of her creations.

"Well, I think you did an absolutely amazing job," Mick gave her a big hug lifting her feet off the floor in the process. "Do they taste as good as they look?"

Lucy nodded vigorously with a cheeky grin. It wasn't hard to see by her exuberance and the icing all over her face that she'd had a few taste tests throughout the afternoon.

"Then I'm guessing you won't need dinner tonight then?" Mick teased her.

"We didn't eat too many," Lucy was a little perturbed at the idea of missing a main meal.

"He's only messing with you Lucy," Sue assured her laughing. "Perhaps you'd better go wash up while we clean up this mess."

"What else did you girls get up to today?" Mick looked around the living room spying a pile of fresh shopping bags from that morning, still laying on the couch. "I see a little more shopping was in order?" He raised his eyebrows to Sue in a teasing way." Just Sue and Lucy today," I said. "I went and joined the gym."

"Really?" Mick was a little in shock. I'm not the type of girl who goes and does exercise. I'm more likely to keep fit by gardening, playing with the dogs, or mucking about at the park with some kids. But when I popped out to the shop for lots of cake mix, I figured I would set myself up for the next stage of recovery. After all, I had a goal, and it was going to require some stamina and strength training.

"Absolutely." I'm pretty proud of myself. "I've signed up with a personal trainer to get me fit and strong again. When she asked for my goal, I told her that I need to get back in the race car… I need strong arms, strong legs and stamina. She was totally wrapped at the idea of me drag racing, and said we'll work up to it slowly as soon as I've recovered from my last chemo. She reckons I should be aiming to have a reasonable fitness level over the next couple of months."

"That's awesome, babe," Mick was right to be sceptical. It was a tad unlikely that I would be able to keep up my gym visits, as I'd never been able to keep up a fitness routine in the past. I've never really had to watch my weight, so hadn't previously had a goal to aim for. But he kept his comments to himself; instead showing encouragement. "Just keep your eye on the goal of handling that high horsepower green machine."

"Absolutely."

"You go girl," Sue was excited to have a girlfriend who drag raced. Well who wouldn't be. It's a pretty cool hobby. But I was not there yet. I still had to get my license, and before I did that, I had to finish my treatment. But for now, the focus was on getting through my very last every chemo. The last time they would ever have to pump that poison through my poor veins.

And again, even after 2 really big days, I still struggled to sleep. Last chemo, last chemo, last chemo …

… No more chemo, no more chemo, no more chemo.

I was excitedly awake bright and early, choosing to get up

as soon as Mick had headed off to work, barely waiting for the sun itself to be up. I really should have stayed in bed, but I couldn't contain myself. I was too excited. It felt like my birthday, and much better than my last birthday when I was recovering from my first ever surgery performed only a couple of days before.

Tip toeing around the house, so as not to wake the girls up, I found the perfect outfit to wear and played with my fake fringe and a few different soft silk scarves under the watchful eye of my dogs, to see which worked best with my celebratory mood.

"Whaddaya doin up so early?" Sue grumbled and headed straight for the kettle to make a coffee. Sue has never been an early morning person.

"I didn't mean to wake you up," I whispered, aware that Lucy was still asleep.

YAWN "It's ok," she managed to get out between yawns. "When do we need to leave?"

"Not for another hour yet. You just chill and have your coffee."

Chapter 20

There's a clinic for that.

Tucked off to the side of King Edward Women's Hospital, there's a few additional clinics that you could be excused in not realising even existed. Until I received my referral in the post for the Menopause Clinic, I was blissfully unaware there was even a need for such a place, but after my first visit I couldn't understand why it wasn't more widely talked about.

I'm sure everyone knows all about menopause, because if they haven't been through it themselves, then their Mum or grandma or auntie has mentioned it as she fans herself with whatever she finds handy in the attempt to cool down on the coldest day in July.

I could stand in an industrial freezer and still have beads of sweat rising up on my upper lip one minute, only to start shivering with cold moments later. Menopause is the reason I wear layers of clothing, ready to peel off or reapply as needed, and the reason that while I really do love a good red wine, I can only partake on the coldest of evenings. It can be the most random of things that will set off a flush, and with equal randomness they disappear making you feel drained and exposed.

I totally understand if any of the fellas reading this choose to skip ahead to the next chapter, because although every woman has to go through it at some point, most men will duck for cover knowing that the temperature variations is only the beginning. Seriously, it's warfare. I've met plenty of women who've said 'sure I went through it without a problem' but when you look at the expression on their loved ones faces, you realise that no-one misses out on the side effects of your youth disappearing in a wave of hot and cold flushes, memory loss and mood swings.

As my particular brand of breast cancer was prone to snacking on estrogen like it was black jellybeans, the first step in my treatment was to stop feeding it, so I was introduced to 'Chemically Induced Menopause'.

If you think menopause is bad, then try multiplying it by ten and you will have the chemically induced big, bad, mean sister.

I should take a moment out to say sorry to everyone anywhere near me at this time, especially Mick who would roll up the edge of the doona and lay it between us in bed as insulation. Even the dogs wouldn't want to lay next to me of an evening due to the amount of heat I would radiate. I swear the neighbours thought I had a bladder problem as my sheets would be so soaked in sweat that I'd have to wash almost every day.

So, when I found out that there was a special clinic that

could help me find various solutions for these side effects, I jumped at the opportunity. I think if I hadn't, Mick would have gone in my place, purely for the sanity of our marriage and to save on the wear and tear of the sheets.

Chapter 21
Ding … You're Cooked

I have my first ever tattoo as an early Christmas present. Actually, I have three of them.

They say when you get a tattoo it should mean something important or be representative of a major event in your life. I've never been against having a tattoo, but I've never found something that I would want drawn on me for the rest of my life either.

So up until now, I've been a clean skin. So, what could be more important and momentous than making it this far in my cancer treatment. It's the perfect event to celebrate with a couple of small tattoos.

So, what did I choose to get tattooed on me to commemorate this special occasion? Three little dots to help the nurses line up the radiation machine the same for every visit, every day for the next five weeks. Well at least I get Christmas Day, Boxing Day and New Year's Day off.

BLIP

I'm mega early for my first appointment, which is just as well, because I got lost trying to work out where the radiation rooms are at the hospital. Here I was thinking they would be somewhere near the doctors or chemo rooms, but it turns out that they have their own little building way, way, way over the other side, away from everything else. But I'm here now, and I've zapped the barcode on my little radiation passport, to check in.

I pull out my book and take a seat in the waiting room. I don't know what to expect, and I'm not even sure I'm in the right place. I see other people come in, zap their barcode and wander off down the hall. They seem to know what they're doing. Maybe I am in the wrong place? What if they've called for me to have my first treatment and I wasn't in the correct room? Would they reschedule my appointment? What if by missing the first appointment I totally mess up the whole routine?

I look up from my book to watch a couple more people walk in the front door ... BLIP ... and off down the hall they go with a sense of self-assurance.

"Excuse me," I've put my book away in my oversized, carry everything handbag and have decided to check with the receptionist. "I've scanned myself in for my first radiation, but I'm not sure if I'm waiting in the right place?"

"You're in the right place," she smiled the biggest and most reassuring smile across the desk. "Someone will come and collect you soon to show you where everything is."

Phew. You know that panic you feel when you think you're in the wrong place, and then the relief when you discover you're in the right place after all? I don't know if I had actually been chilling out in the wrong waiting room or not, but no sooner had I resat down when a nurse came and collected me for my own personal one on one tour of the radiation rooms.

"Each time you arrive, you'll scan yourself in like you did today, but you can then head for the Banksia Room," she let me know as we walked down the hall passing several smaller semi-enclosed waiting rooms, each named after an Australian wildflower, and each with their own calming fish tank room divider.

"Everyone has their own locker which in your case will always have a gown available for you." She grabbed the gown out of my locker, picked up a little shopping basket from the collection, and directed me towards the change rooms. "If there's any change in your schedule, or the doctor needs to see you, we'll put a note in your locker."

"So, when you arrive, grab your gown, get changed, and then wait in the Banksia waiting room until you're called. Once you're done, you can get changed, put your gown back in the locker, and head home. All to be repeated again the next day until you're done."

"Awesome," I said, somewhat apprehensively. I grabbed up the basket and my gown and headed to the change rooms to get this new routine started.

So tomorrow I would be one of those self-assured people

walking in, scanning their barcode and heading off down the hall, knowing that they had a locker and shopping basket sitting there waiting for them. But today, I was feeling and even smelling like a fish out of water.

As per instructions, I had showered but not put on any deodorant, makeup, perfume, creams or oils. But that was hours ago, and I've not only had a nervous sweat happening due to the thought I'd totally messed up my whole appointment by waiting in the wrong waiting room, I was also going through chemically induced menopause. I wasn't smelling very fresh at all, so keeping this in mind, I chose to sit the furthest away from everyone else in the new smaller waiting room with the calming fish tank room divider.

Have you ever noticed that all the really important machines at the hospital are shaped like giant donuts with sliding beds in the middle?

And the rooms that they're housed in, seem to be a lot bigger than they need to be and are very cold. At least they are much too cold when you're asked to remove half your clothing which for some reason when you get scans you don't have to, but for radiation you do.

The waiting room was carefully designed with its neutral coloured carpet and calming fish tank, but once I was through that "warning radioactive area" tape, it was purely business. Well almost, as I'd begun to realise everywhere through the cancer treatment rooms, nurses seem to have a more relaxed attitude.

Behind the giant glass viewing window - which made me feel like I was on display in a zoo - behind the row of computer screens in charge of controlling how long I'd be in the microwave, there were smiling faces, friendly voices, and some pretty cool music.

"Take a deep breath, and hoooooooooooooold," said one of those disembodied voices once they had me lying as still as possible, partially naked, head to one side, arms above my head, inside the donut. "... and breathe normally again."

I think I was expecting fluro green lasers and zapping noises, but instead it was just like being inside a giant x-ray machine. There wasn't even a BING at the end of my microwave session to say I was done. How disappointing. I think this is certainly a modification that needs to be considered.

"OK, you're done," came the voice as the bed lowered down. After all that preparation, worry, and waiting, I had spent barely ten minutes being zapped. Although laying in that awkward position made it feel much longer in muscle memory time.

"See you tomorrow," the smiling nurse showed me back out through the warning tape to the change rooms.

Day one, done and dusted. Only twenty-four sessions left to go of driving thirty minutes to the hospital, being zapped in the giant microwave for 10 minutes, and then driving 30 minutes home again.

Only twenty-three to go ... Only twenty-two to go ... only twenty-one to go ...

Only four zaps in the giant microwave to go, and although I'm feeling itchy and looking a bit blotchy, I'm happy to say I'm not looking like the burnt piece of toast like I was expecting. I simply look like I've been hanging out at Swanborne nudist beach with my shirt open only on one side.

Only one zap left ... it's time to hand in my passport and say farewell to the fish.

Chapter 22
Barbie Foobs

Waking up in my own private room with an elephant sitting on my chest, four drainage tubes attached to four bottles of floaty bits, and a cannula in my foot, I am pretty apprehensive about what I'm going to see under those hospital sheets. I should preface this by saying I am on a good quantity of morphine, and I haven't moved much yet, but on taking that first peek under the sheets I really did expect to see loads of bandages. I thought my whole chest would be wrapped up in an overzealous boob tube made of gauze making me look like some half wrapped up Egyptian mummy. But instead all I see is two rather large mounds covered in surgical tape and lots of purple texta markings. What is it with plastic surgeons and their textas? Surely, it's about time someone invested in body markers like you have whiteboard markers that easily rub off.

These swollen lumps don't actually look like boobs, but I'm still pleasantly surprised at how clean and tidy my newly created foobs look. Yep, that's the new word for them, my fake boobs are now foobs.

I give them a very gentle poke, being careful not to cause any pain, but they're hard as rocks and the skin is stretched tighter than a drum skin. No wonder I felt like I was in some kind of compression vest. My surgeon appeared to have stuffed as much silicone into what was left of the old breast skin as possible. We discussed going down in size, but I think he must have changed his mind while I was under. Or maybe Mick had a word with him on the sly. These definitely look bigger than the old girls, but lying on my back, the old girls wouldn't have been standing up like this, so it was hard to judge.

"Send me a picture." If you haven't already guessed, this was Sue also expecting to see chest carnage.

"There's really not much to see," I told her. By this point I had managed to almost sit up with the aid of the motorised hospital bed and change out of the surgery gown into my standard hospital garb of a flannel shirt, but the tracky pants would have to wait until I had the cannula removed from my foot. Because the surgeon was working on both sides to give me two new boobies, the anaesthetist had no other choice than to go into the top of my foot. It wasn't as bad as I thought it would be, but that might also be due to the amount of medication I was still on. What it did cause a problem with was wearing pants, but it wasn't like I was going to be jogging laps of the ward just yet, so I kept the hospital gown on under the blankets with one foot poking out and attached to the happy juice.

"Besides, you're coming down to Perth to look after me

when I get out of here in a week anyway," I reminded her. Sue had been there for all the big moments during my treatment, and new boobs was one that she particularly didn't want to miss out on.

"Absolutely, I'm going to be your nurse and change your dressings and stuff. But that's a whole week away, and you're in a private room, so just open up and take a picture," she encouraged me.

"I'll try, but I can't move much." Even though I was on some pretty good pain meds, I was still finding it a bit of a struggle to move. Getting up to go to the toilet or have a shower so I could wash off all this purple texta was definitely out of the question, so sitting up to take a selfie was certainly going to be an effort.

"OK, OK, as soon as I get off the phone then. I'll send you photos of my four drains, the canula in my foot and then my new boobies." The things you do for your good friends.

True to my word, I'm sitting propped up on a pillow, shirt open, phone in selfie mode poised about to take the photo when the nurse walks into my room to check on me. Talk about awkward moment. I suddenly felt like a teenage boy when his Mum walks in the bedroom.

"What are you doing?"

"My friend who lives out of town, wants to see the result." I tried not to laugh while I was telling her because even on morphine, laughing would be painful. But the look on her face was too priceless, and I couldn't help but have a very gentle giggle at the absurdity of it all.

"I'll leave you to it then," and with that she left the room with the episode never spoken of again. I'm sure it made the conversation at the nurses' desk though. But I'm also sure I'm not the first to take post-surgery photos to send to their odd besties.

Little did I realise that I wouldn't really get this opportunity again, as shortly after, I was strapped into the straight jacket style compression bra. Way back when I went for my first ever bra fitting with my Mum, in that private out of the way lingerie store in the city, I would never have imagined that there was such a garment as a post-surgery compression bra. Trying it on for only a few minutes, weeks before my surgery to remove my existing tainted boobs and replace them with shiny new ones, gave me absolutely no idea of how uncomfortable a bra could actually be.

"If you want to have a good final result, you'll need to wear this all the time," the breast nurse told me very matter of factly. "After all, you are carrying around 600ml on each side, so while you might not notice it at first, they can stretch and drop." Ew, the thought of having saggy fake boobs was enough to have me convinced.

"What exactly do you mean by ALL the time?" I asked.

"I mean for the next eight weeks you only take it off to have a shower," she said.

There's very little that can be planned for or scheduled around your day to day life when you're dealing with cancer treatment, especially when you're working within the public health system, trying to run your own business, and preparing to race a drag car for the first time. So when

I did a quick calculation in my head, working out that the compression bra should be off around the end of August, and the pre-racing season test and tunes would be in October I was pretty excited about this journey being near the end.

"Will my foobs be OK to be strapped into a racing harness by October?" I asked the surgeon when he popped by to have a look at his handywork.

"Medically they'll be fine," he laughed at my eagerness to get back into driver training. "They won't burst under the pressure or anything like that, you just might find it a little uncomfortable for a while." I couldn't imagine anything being more uncomfortable than this zip up bra, but I wasn't going to let that stop me.

It seemed so long ago since I'd been practicing my launches and burnouts in Gonzo's driveway, and even though I couldn't physically practice with the car running, I had been going through each routine familiarising myself with the process of racing a pretty quick drag car.

Not only had I been visiting the workshop to sit in the driver's seat, but I also had a photo of the dash setup on my computer at home and each step written out clearly on giant pieces of butcher's paper hung on the wall. I was determined that nothing was getting in the way of me racing this time. It had been too long coming.

Chapter 23
I'm a Race Car Driver

Well, it all finally happened. It's been a couple of years since Mick and I bought that little Green Torana, and everything has tried to stand in our way of getting it down the track. But together we stood firm with a common goal in mind. Whatever happens, the aim was just to get me to drive the Torana at a ridiculous speed down that drag strip. Regardless of how long it was going to take, and how long the Torana had to sit there and wait, the goal was never changing.

When I started my cancer appointments and contacts diary, I took the advice from some of the ladies in my support group, and put a couple of inspirational pictures on the first page. Unlike many other patients who choose to have pictures of family or pets, I had two of the Torana. One of it launching off the start line with the previous owner behind the wheel, and the other sitting at the workshop with me as its new owner. When the journey got tough and I was starting to lose focus I could look at that page and remind myself of the amazingly exciting future I still had waiting for me. And I wasn't shy in showing every doctor and nurse on my team that they were an integral part of this process. I was the one doing the fighting, but it was up to them to provide me with all the right tools. They were a big part of helping me reach my goal.

***

I feel sick.

I am finally sitting in the driver's seat, my helmet is on tight, the race harness is firmly holding those brand new boobies in place, and ahead of me through the race tunnel I can see the long black strip of the drag racing track. There are track officials everywhere, all with their eyes on me. Mick is standing at the front of the car nervously pumping his squirty bottle of methanol, poised in readiness to start the car. Gonzo is standing off to one side, excitedly grinning at the fact that we really are about to do this after so long and after so many delays.

Other racers and crew members take the opportunity to come by and wish me luck. It's hugs and thumbs up from everyone. They all seem to have so much confidence in me, but I just feel sick.

I am starting to sweat under my thick fireproof race suit, and my visor and glasses are fogging up with my heavy breathing. I only have to start the car and do a burnout for the first part of my license, but suddenly I can't remember what to do. This is a purpose-built race car, it's not a case of simply turning the key, giving it a little accelerator and then off you go.

The track official gives a thumbs up. We're ready for my first licensing test.

I feel sick.

Gonzo gives Mick the thumbs up and I take a deep shaky breath and try to picture the steps I have written out on the butchers' paper above my desk at home. Check I'm in neutral, pull the fuel lever all the way, switch the power on, watch for Mick to spray fuel into the engine, and CRANK IT…

The smell of race fuel fills the cabin, and the sound of that small block engine roars through my earplugs. My eyeballs are vibrating, or maybe that's just the Perspex window and my helmet visor. I place my shaky right hand on the gear stick and the left on the steering wheel. Clunk her into first gear and carefully roll through the tunnel … let's do this.

Off to one side I can see a track official spraying water onto the burnout pad while Mick runs ahead and guides me into position. Ever so slowly, terrified that I will overshoot the mark, I creep the car into position. I can hear my heart beating over the sound of the engine, and my erratic breathing is fogging up my helmet and glasses.

"You can do this," I whisper to myself. "Just focus on one step at a time."

The track official points to Mick. Mick points to me and starts circling his hand.

My right foot slams the accelerator to the floor, my left knee is locked in place holding the brake. Smoke starts to fill the cabin as I fight with the steering wheel to keep this powerful beast pointing forward. I don't feel sick anymore, and I'm shaking but it's no longer nerves.

I start rolling through to the start line, while Mick runs ahead and waves for me to settle down. It's not over yet, but if I go in too fast, I'll miss my opportunity. I only have to watch the lights count down and then launch. There are no other cars on the track, but I am being watched and judged by the officials in red shirts.

"You can do this," I'm talking to myself again. "It's the same as you practiced in Gonzo's driveway. Head back, hands in position, eyes on the lights, and …"

Was that green? Nothing is happening. WOAH that's full on, I forgot about the delay. Oh damn! my foot slipped. Never mind just pedal it again. Oh, that's right I'm supposed to gently drive to the end of the track.

Getting out at the end of the track, waiting for the guys to come and collect me in the tow car, I can't help but think about how I totally messed up my first attempt on the track. But I also can't help but think about how awesome it was to be there in the first place. And I don't have to get it right straight away, we have plenty of test and tune days left.

So around we went, again and again and again until finally the officials in their red shirts signed my license book. By the end of the day I had managed to do a 9.10 second full track pass, crossing the finish line at 147mph. Not bad for a girl who had never done a burnout before or even driven a V8. Bring on the race season, I'm ready to race against other cars.

Chapter 24

I Won.

I Won!!!! I'm through to the next round of racing. How did I manage that?

"The other racer jumped the start and red lit, so by default, you win," I was reliably informed by my crew when they arrived at the top of the track to collect me after my first competition race.

"Cool," I beamed. "A win is a win. I'll take it."

And then an hour later, waiting at the top of the track I see my crew driving up to me cheering.

"Again?"

I was incredulous that in my first ever competition event I was managing to win races. I have been around drag racing enough to know that this was a fairly unique turn of events, but still very possible for someone to keep achieving wins by default. After all, in drag racing you have to make it to the start line under your own power, can't leave before the green light, you can't cross the white line and you can't go faster than you said you would. So, because all the other racers seemed to be having a bad day, I was making it through rounds of racing.

"Just think of it as more practice rounds," suggested Gonzo when I mentioned that as we were reaching the pointy end of the night, I was getting quite nervous about people's expectations of my skill level. I still wasn't feeling very confident out there, and as the dew started to settle on the track and I began to get weary regardless of the amount of adrenaline running through my veins, my inexperience showed.

But still to the surprise and excitement of everyone I kept winning rounds. Until that very last one almost ten hours after my very first race.

"And as Paul Downe lines up against Andy Kahle for the Super Sedan finals. This is Andy's first event having only just got her license a week ago." I can't hear the commentator over the PA. Even if he could be heard above the roar of my little V8 engine, my concentration was entirely on Mick who is standing off to my left in front of me getting ready to wind up my last burnout of the night.

Regardless of what happens during this race, this is it. After beginning the day with over thirty competitors I am now one of the final two left in the competition.

I open my eyes as wide as possible, my right foot slams the accelerator to the floor, my left knee is locked in place holding the brake.

Smoke starts to fill the cabin and I fight with the steering wheel for the last time that night. As I pull out of the burnout, and reset the car ready for race mode, Mick runs up to the start line ready to help me in place.

I have a routine now to help calm myself down.

I take a deep breath, check all my levers and switches are in the correct on or off position, then very, very gently roll the Torana up to the first of the two starting line beams. I take another deep and slow breath, close my visor all the way, look straight down the track at the finish line, and then open my eyes as wide as they can go, refuse to blink and roll into full stage.

GO, GO, GO …

"Well done, thanks for a great race," Paul was shaking my hand after the finish line. Sure, he'd won the race, but I'm not sure if he knew how much of a winner I was just by being there. I didn't need the runner up trophy that I was presented with later that night after we'd packed up the car and cracked a couple of cans to celebrate.

As I climbed the podium with my post chemo curly hair, to say thank you for all the support I've received, the previous eighteen months simply welled up inside. There were so many people who had the confidence that I would make it to this point, but I knew when I was handed the microphone and my runner up trophy that if I said much more than a quick thank you that I would end up becoming a cry baby again. But this time with tears of overwhelming joy and appreciation.

I'd won.

No more drugs, no more radiation, no more surgery.

No more cancer.

Chapter 25
Just the Beginning

Sitting here recapping this small but far from insignificant point of my life some ten years later, and still totally cancer free, I have come across memories that have been very difficult to share and others that I chose not to. I fully understand that for many they will be difficult and perhaps even painful to read. But I do hope that while there have been some very serious and sombre moments, you did find plenty to get you laughing or rolling your eyes in the way Mick does so often at me now.

"You want to do what now?" he sighs with the exasperation- only a long-suffering husband whose wife has rediscovered the joy of life can understand.

"Fine, just try not to hurt yourself, or at least give me some warning if I need to up your life insurance," he jokes.

After my journey, I've noticed that people look at me in a different way. It's not that sympathy or pity look in their eyes any more like I used to see while I was going through treatment, there's something different there now. They think they are simply seeing someone who is confident and happy with her lot in life, but I know they're really seeing someone with a whole new attitude. It's the kind of attitude that only a person who's been through a life changing experience can really understand.

It might be an unusual thing to say, but I do consider myself to be very lucky to have had this experience. It's like a fog has been lifted and I can see what I'm supposed to do with my life, and how to enjoy every minute of it. Just set your mind to something, grab life by the balls and go out there and do it. Don't let anything hold you back.

You only get one life, and it's pretty short.

So, don't waste it on anything or anyone who doesn't make you feel you are the best person you can possibly be.

NOT THE END YET ...

See you at the racetrack.

*While I have cried for so many friends
whom I've lost
and those who are still struggling to survive,
I am reminded that a true friend
lives forever in your heart.
In your heart they will always be strong,
healthy and smiling.*

*Do not grieve ...
remember them and smile. :)*

www.ingramcontent.com/pod-product-compliance
Lightning Source LLC
Chambersburg PA
CBHW070255010526
44107CB00056B/2467